Growing Irises

Tetraploid Louisiana 'Magistral'

Growing Irises

Graeme Grosvenor

SECOND EDITION

Kangaroo Press

Acknowledgments

The author would like to express his gratitude to Bob Raabe for the prints of his iris 'Magistral' and 'Milk Maid'; to Barry Blyth for the slides of 'Baghdad Note Sib', 'For Pleasure', 'Ben Abou', 'Jewelled Veil', 'Making Eyes', 'Sundown Red', 'Inner Circle', 'Ego', three slides of Californian iris, 'Cabaret Royale', 'French Gown', 'Magic Man' and 'Bluebird Wine'; to Kim Blaxland for the slides of *Laevigata albopurpurea monstrosa, Iris foetidissima, iris unguicularis* 'Wisome' and reticulata iris; to Lloyd Woolnough for the slide of 'Brookvale Nocturne'; to Helen Grosvenor for typing the manuscript; to Pam Boyle for the line drawings; and in particular to John Taylor who helped so much in the preparation of the author's slides, who read, corrected, read again and continued to correct the manuscript, who prepared all the diagrams and line drawings in association with Pam Boyle and who has supported him in all his efforts in preparing this book.

Front Cover: 'First Movement' (tall bearded iris). Pure rich apricot bred by the author. This early blooming iris is a seedling from 'Words and Music' and is an Award of Merit winner (p.22).

Second edition published in 1992
First published in 1984 by Kangaroo Press
3 Whitehall Road (P.O. Box 75) Kenthurst 2156
Typeset by G.T. Setters Pty Limited
Printed in Hong Kong by Colorcraft Ltd

ISBN 0 86417 442 X

Contents

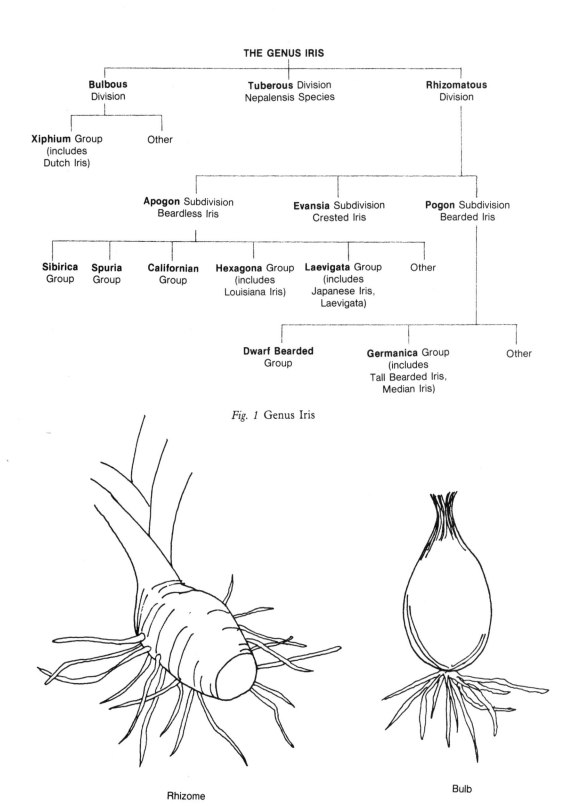

THE GENUS IRIS

Bulbous Division

Tuberous Division
Nepalensis Species

Rhizomatous Division

Xiphium Group
(includes
Dutch Iris)

Other

Apogon Subdivision
Beardless Iris

Evansia Subdivision
Crested Iris

Pogon Subdivision
Bearded Iris

Sibirica Group

Spuria Group

Californian Group

Hexagona Group
(includes
Louisiana Iris)

Laevigata Group
(includes
Japanese Iris,
Laevigata)

Other

Dwarf Bearded Group

Germanica Group
(includes
Tall Bearded Iris,
Median Iris)

Other

Fig. 1 Genus Iris

Rhizome

Bulb

Fig. 2 Rhizome *vs* bulb

Introduction

Anyone with any interest in plants and gardens and indeed many with no such interest at all are aware of the great range of iris available to the gardener. In recent years hybridisers have achieved amazing improvements in flower and colour. This book is aimed at bringing the iris, the rainbow flower, to the attention of all who would enhance their gardens with its incomparable beauty of flower shape and colour.

In Greek mythology Iris was the goddess of the rainbow. As she watches over irisarians of today she must often have a quiet chuckle at the author, now her most devoted servant. I well remember observing, as a young boy, a large patch of the old purple-flowered 'Kharput' or *Iris germanica* growing around a camellia tree in my grandparents' home in Sydney. It flowered well enough but neither the rich purple colour nor the form appealed to me. I thought its brief period of bloom meant that it was a waste of good garden space, and space was valuable on a small inner city block.

When the house came into my hands, many years later, the old purple 'Kharput' was still in the garden. True to my word I very quickly disposed of it; the camellia remained but an ancient fig, a mulberry tree and an apple tree quickly followed the iris to make way for my beloved roses and azaleas.

Now several years and two moves of houses later I find myself with a large and still increasing collection of iris and in the position of running an iris nursery. I have become an avid hybridiser, importer and exporter of iris and I share these interests with friends in many parts of the world. Oh, how the goddess must chuckle! **Plates 1-6**

I first came to growing iris when I was seeking a companion plant for roses. (Is there such a thing?) I read that tall bearded iris enjoyed the same conditions and came in a large range of colours. I bought a collection from Sunnyside Gardens—later to become Tempo Two Nursery—and well remember my joy when the first iris bloomed. I had never seen anything like it before. The flower's colour was brown stitching on a white background and the iris was named 'Rocket Rust'; in retrospect not particularly well grown.

However, I was hooked; more and more flowered and more and more were purchased.

In the past much of the hybridising of iris has centred on the United States with considerable European interest in bearded iris. The development of the Dutch Iris for the florists' trade in Holland and the development of the *Kaempferi* (or Japanese) iris in Japan kept these countries in the forefront of iris nations.

Interest in iris has led to the formation of national iris societies in the United States, England, France, Germany, Italy, South Africa and Switzerland. In recent years there has been an explosion of interest in Australia and New Zealand and both countries have very active iris societies.

Iris societies present a marvellous opportunity for people to share with others their experiences in the pleasures of growing and, for some, the showing of iris. Having formed many friendships in this way I had no reservations in saying yes when given the opportunity to write this book and perhaps introduce others to the pleasures of growing iris.

Iris can be grown throughout Australia and New Zealand and although there are some areas where individual species and individual cultivars will fail there is an iris suitable for your garden wherever you live. As well as the species (in excess of 200) there are the iridaceae or iris-like plants which are not discussed in this book but about which a separate book could be written. Many of the iridaceae are natives of the southern hemisphere, in particular South Africa, while the iris species are nearly exclusively native to the northern hemisphere. An exception to the latter rule is the Australian native *Patersonia* with its fleeting blue-purple flowers. It is unfortunately of little use as a cultivated plant.

Plants of the genus Iris are perennials typified by having floral parts in sets of three. The genus can be set into two main divisions—bulbous and rhizomatous. A third division, referred to as Nepalensis Iris, is not discussed in this book. For those interested, a discussion of this latter division of iris can be found in The American Iris Society's *The World of Iris* edited by Bee

Warburton. Figure 1 sets out the broad divisions of the genus Iris and Figure 2 indicates the nature of differences in plant structure. In this book I will attempt to avoid as much as possible excessive use of botanic names which are often difficult to pronounce and almost impossible to spell. So don't be put off by the classification given in Figure 1.

The rhizomatous iris can be set into three sub-divisions—*Pogoniris* or bearded iris, *Apogoniris* or beardless iris, and *Evansia* or crested iris. Within the divisions of bearded, beardless and crested iris there are many subdivisions. For the bearded iris this subgrouping is largely based on the height of the flowering spikes. Chapter 2 discusses the largest of these subgroups—the tall bearded iris. This is followed by a chapter on other bearded iris.

Following chapters are devoted to the crested iris and to the most popular of the beardless iris, that is, those iris where there are numerous hybrids readily available to the interested gardener—for example, the Louisiana iris, Spuria iris, Siberian iris and Japanese iris—the one exception being a separate chapter on Californian iris, even though named hybrids are now only just becoming available. One further chapter is devoted to that all-encompassing group, other beardless iris.

Chapter 8 is devoted to the bulbous iris. These are the only iris really suited to the florists' trade and as such form a multi-million dollar worldwide business.

Accompanying each chapter is a list of recommended iris. These are iris of quality—proven varieties commercially available in 1992. In time some, no doubt, will be surpassed and slip from favour but at the time of writing they are the best available.

Figure 3 indicates the bloom period and the sequence of bloom for the main types of iris discussed in this book. By growing several types of iris a long and varied bloom season can be achieved.

Several miscellaneous chapters complete the book. These cover such things as hybridising iris, iris societies and their awards, purchasing iris, photographing iris, exhibiting and arranging iris. A glossary is also included to provide an easy reference for terms which may not be familiar to readers new to growing iris.

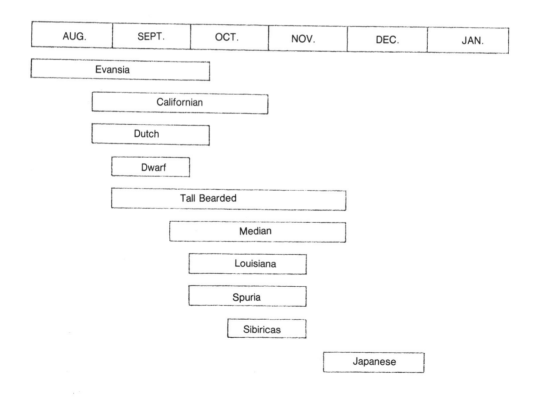

Fig. 3 Bloom period

1. Tall Bearded Iris

As a general rule bearded iris can be classified by the height of the plants' flower spike, as indicated in Figure 4. The tall bearded iris (TBs) have been and still remain the most popular and best known of the iris family. TBs are tough, hardy perennials which will survive the worst neglect but are most responsive and rewarding when given the attention they deserve.

It is useful to split a discussion of TBs into three sections. First, the plant and its growth cycle; second, the flowering stalk or spike; and third, the flower.

Growing TB Iris

In relation to the plant, the desirable traits in modern tall bearded iris are:

1. *Vigour*—this involves the production of large strong rhizomes which are able to provide tall flowering spikes. Further, the rhizomes must multiply readily providing a good foundation for an increasing quantity of bloom in coming years.

2. *Health*—the iris should be disease-resistant and capable of adjusting to the normal problems of weather.

3. *Foliage*—apart from maintaining a good appearance as a result of resistance to disease the iris should not produce foliage at the expense of flowering spikes nor should it 'bloom-out', that is, the over-production of flowers which leaves the plant without increase to form the basis of flowering in following years.

To achieve the most from growing TBs the gardener should be aware of the growth cycle of the rhizome. Bearded iris flower in mid-spring, so mid-October can be taken as the average flowering time in the southern hemisphere. After the flowering period the iris plant goes into a period of active growth followed by semi-dormancy in mid to late summer. A rhizome, once it has flowered, will not flower again and all its energy is put into developing increase, that is, new rhizomes that will flower in the following season. These increase, which first appear in late summer, are the normal means of propagating iris. The increase develop from the original rhizome as illustrated in Figure 5. The

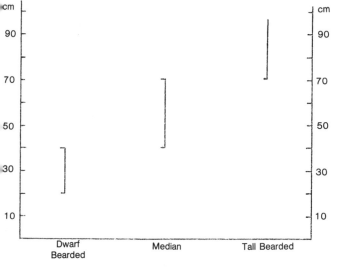

Fig. 4 Height classification of bearded iris

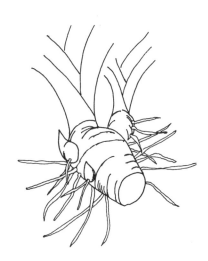

Fig. 5 Rhizome and increase

First year plant with the bloom stalk removed and new growth starting for the following season

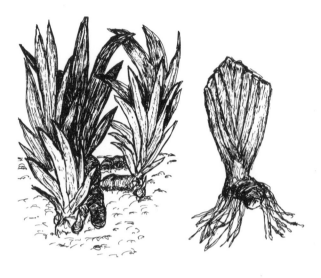

Fig. 6 Dividing up an old clump

characteristics of the daughter plants will be exactly the same as those of the parent rhizome.

Rhizomes that have not flowered develop rapidly in the early summer; new root growth is followed by a swelling of the rhizome and luxuriant foliage growth. Obviously the best time to plant rhizomes or divide established clumps is during the mid to late summer dormancy which immediately follows the growth period. It can be difficult to know exactly when the switch from active growth to semi-dormancy occurs, although this is not critical and planting in the southern hemisphere can be completed any time from November through to early May. In my view the best times are early December and late February to early March. Early planting is recommended to ensure good growth and flowering in the following year.

As already stated, each individual rhizome will flower only once and then put its energy into producing increase for the following year's bloom. Once this increase has been made the 'mother' rhizome is of no further use and tends to clutter up the clump. This is no problem in the first one or two years after planting but in future years the clump extends radially with an increasingly large 'dead' centre (see Figure 6).

The most usual complaint heard from gardeners about their iris is: 'they flowered well in the first couple of years but they didn't flower this year.' This is often a result of lack of knowledge of the growth cycle. Although there is no hard and fast rule, digging and

replanting are essential parts of iris growing. As a general rule a clump of tall bearded iris should have reached its peak after three years. It is then time to divide and replant. Failure to do this will often result in deterioration in quality and quantity of bloom even if a rigid fertilising campaign is maintained. Extremely quick increasers and vigorous growers may need division after only two years. Less vigorous varieties could remain in the ground up to five years. Much of the pleasure of growing iris is getting to know your cultivars and coaxing the best results from them.

If a plant fails in a particular part of the garden there is every possibility that moving it to another place in the garden will produce the desired result. There are many examples of iris which do spectacularly well in some gardens while performing dismally in other gardens in the same area. Fortunately there are those universally great iris which perform well everywhere and these are the cultivars recommended for the beginner or the iris enthusiast who has room for only a few plants.

Because of the habit of growth of the tall bearded iris the best plants are to be found on the edge of the clump, so when dividing select only the best and strongest rhizomes for replanting and discard the rest. Having selected the best rhizomes trim back the foliage, leaving no more than 20cm of growth, and then trim back the roots, leaving about 5–6cm. (When purchasing new plants this will be done for you by

Established clumps ready for dividing

Lifting a clump

A plant ready to send out

11

the nursery.) Excessive root growth is unnecessary as the old roots die off only to be replaced by new growth and the cutting back of foliage serves a twofold purpose—it prevents the plant being moved about by the elements but more importantly leaves less foliage for the rhizomes to support while the all-important root growth proceeds.

Proximity of rhizomes to each other at planting time is really a question for the individual, as individual gardeners will decide whether they want a massed effect, with the inevitable need to divide earlier, or whether each clump should be slowly established and appreciated for its own beauty. Good rhizomes planted at the right time should produce at least one flowering spike with anything from 6 to 15 or more flowers in the first season. Adequate growth and increase would give 3 to 6 flowering spikes in the second season if the clump is not divided. Yearly division and replanting will inevitably produce more flowering plants but flower quality may suffer in some cultivars. There are some cultivars which resent moving and will not flower in the first year. Nearly always these produce a large clump and bloom beautifully in the second year. These varieties are best handled by taking one or more plants from the outside of the clump each year to ensure both continuous bloom and satisfactory increase.

To grow TB iris for the beauty of the individual clump established over a period of three or four years, the rhizomes should be planted anything from 60cm to 90cm apart. A display can be achieved more quickly by planting three rhizomes in a triangular pattern 30cm apart. For a massed display 10 to 12 rhizomes of a single cultivar can be planted or colours blended or contrasted.

Soil Preparation

Soil preparation is an essential prerequisite to growing iris well. The better the soil condition the better are plants established. Although tall bearded iris are very tolerant of a wide range of soil conditions, the best soil for them is a medium to heavy loam, slightly alkaline and well drained. Iris are heavy feeders and the soil should be as fertile as possible. Let me hasten to add, however, that many beautiful blooms have been produced in sandy soils and in soils that are less than perfect.

Not only do iris grow better in alkaline soil but it has been shown by experiments in the US that the foliage is more luxuriant and the annoying brown tips found on the foliage of some plants avoidable if tall bearded iris are grown in good soil conditions.

Sandy soil can be improved by the addition of animal manures but care must be taken to use only well-rotted manure and to incorporate it into the soil beneath where the rhizome is to be planted. Using young or 'hot' manure placed around or on the rhizome can induce a disease known as rhizome rot. (This disease is discussed further below.)

Increase in alkalinity can be achieved by adding lime to the soil at the rate of about a handful to the square metre, or better still by adding both calcium and magnesium salts by using dolomite at the same rate. At the same time the addition of a chemical fertiliser in the N:P:K range of 6:10:6 or thereabouts is very beneficial. If this exact formula is unobtainable, any close approximation is satisfactory as long as the nitrogen content is controlled. Over-supply of nitrogen causes soft, sappy and often luxuriant growth, sometimes to the detriment of flowers, and it can induce rhizome rot, but it is an unwise gardener who totally cuts out the supply of nitrogen because of a potential negative reaction to its use.

Planting

No matter how the iris are used in the landscape the mechanics of planting are always the same (see Figure 7). After digging a hole large enough to accommodate the rhizome a mound of soil is made to about 2cm below ground level. The rhizome is placed on the mound and the roots used to anchor the plant. This should ensure that the top of the rhizome is approximately at ground level. Care should be taken to ensure

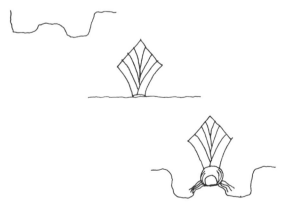

Fig. 7 Planting bearded iris

Preparing the ground

Planting the iris

that the 'toe' or pointed part of the rhizome (most distant from the foliage) is well anchored into the ground. Failure to do so will often result in dry rot (discussed below). Great success both in promoting growth and reducing the incidence of rhizome rot has been achieved by incorporating a slow release fertiliser of the 8–9 month type at the rate of a small handful to each rhizome in the soil at planting time. This fertiliser, working on the principle of osmosis, releases a small amount of nutriment with watering over the full growing period up to flowering the following season if the 8–9 month type is used. Although some of these fertilisers are a little high in nitrogen content, results are very good.

Most of the cultural work associated with the growing of tall bearded iris is completed at planting time; reference to the growth pattern of the rhizome is needed to clarify future requirements. If soil preparation is adequate and the planting and initial fertilising instructions are followed there is no need for further fertilising until late in the following winter when, in most areas, growth is again initiated.

After a period of rapid growth and the formation of baby rhizomes in the later summer and autumn the growth slows with the approach of colder weather. The plants are winter dormant. Much is to be gained by watering well during the late summer and autumn months, but with the approach of dormancy the water supply should be cut down and very little if any artificial watering is required in the winter months. In late winter the iris should be fertilised with a 6:10:6 chemical fertiliser and the new growth encouraged by again increasing the supply of water. The only other fertilising required (again with a 6:10:6 chemical) is a boost along for established iris after flowering time.

Summarising and simplifying these procedures— water the plants when they are actively growing and withdraw water when they are dormant, fertilise in November/December and again in August. Iris are gross feeders and easy of cultivation so it is difficult to make mistakes by over-attending to their needs—in general they respond to any extra care and attention they are given.

Pests and Diseases

In the southern hemisphere gardeners are fortunate that most of the diseases that can cause difficulty in iris growing and plague northern hemisphere growers just do not exist. Our rigid quarantine laws have ensured the propagation of good stock from imported rhizomes while there are several active local hybridisers producing plants of outstanding quality. It seems that iris are just about universally infected with a virus of some form or other and particular cultivars show a great difference in reaction to the viruses. Some tolerant tall bearded iris show no visible symptoms of virus at all while others show varying amounts of striation and mottling. The symptoms are always more pronounced in cooler weather. Many varieties show no symptoms at all in summer but have mottled foliage in spring and autumn. Again the appearance of the plant may vary from season to season.

At the time of writing no cure for the common mosaic virus has been found. Only plants which are tolerant should be grown and badly infected plants should be destroyed. No reputable nurseryman will sell badly infected plants showing low tolerance and as the plants are universally infected little can be done. It is believed that the mosaic virus is transmitted from one plant to another by aphids so control of aphids could help control the spread of the virus. The floral parts, while infected, do not usually show any visible sign of virus. Occasional petal flecking may occur (many find this an attractive diversion) and on rare

occasions the flower may be distorted or deformed.

An interesting experience of the author's is with the tall bearded iris 'Splash O' Wine' (Plate 56). This beautiful and prolific rose burgundy on creamy white plicata flowered for several seasons without showing any sign of virus in the home garden at West Pennant Hills. Winters there are frosty and there was never any winter rebloom. Upon being moved to the nursery site at Dural, a distance of less than 10 kilometres but with milder winters and very little frost, 'Splash O' Wine' has been a consistent winter rebloomer but has often thrown the odd distorted flower, although only in winter. Spring bloom remains beautiful and 'Splash O' Wine' is a very popular iris.

Another common disease is fungal leaf spot, which can appear as small circular spots which darken to yellow and brown and often enlarge. Severe infection can see the whole leaf become brown and unsightly and the leaf will usually die back from the tip. Although this disease is not fatal it is most unsightly and, as with most fungal infections, prevention is better than cure.

The fungus spores live in the soil or on dead or previously infected leaves and the fungus becomes a

Iris leaves showing leaf spot and virus (streaks in foliage)

14

problem in wet weather, particularly if it is humid as well. Clean cultivation is the best preventative so all dead and any diseased leaves should be removed. When the disease is noticed, the foliage showing infection should be cut back and burned and the healthy foliage and soil around the plant sprayed with a suitable fungicide such as Benlate, Maneb, Zineb or Mancozeb. The author uses Dithane M45, a Mancozeb compound, with very satisfactory results.

Iris rust is a similar fungal disease, not as common as leaf spot, brought on by similar climatic conditions and treated in the same way as leaf spot.

Pineappling is a mystery disease peculiar to the bearded iris. The rhizome becomes enlarged, the foliage stunted and pleated and flowering stems are either non-existent or very short and malformed. The rhizome often does not make increase and there is no known cure. As the disease is more prevalent in warmer, more humid climates, it is the author's *opinion* that it is a result of the iris not acclimatising. This is supported by the fact that clumps can improve from one year to the next, but rarely deteriorate, and that, at times, only one of several newly planted rhizomes is affected. The disease is usually noted in iris planted for the first time and coming from a colder climate to a warmer climate. Pineappling is not common and is best treated by removing the affected rhizome and replanting with new stock. Any reputable nurseryman will replace free of charge newly purchased stock so affected.

By far the worst disease affecting tall bearded iris is bacterial soft rot. While normally not fatal it can, under certain circumstances, wipe out a whole iris clump. Soft rot starts where the leaf fan meets the rhizome and can be accompanied by yellowing of foliage and the death of the leaf fans. In advanced stages the rhizome becomes a spongy mass which gives off a foul odour.

Soft rot, which is quite common, is prevalent in wet and humid weather in spring, summer and autumn. Some cultivars are prone to the disease while others are never affected. The most often affected iris are the vigorous sappy growers, so prevention is helped by keeping the nitrogen supply low.

In the author's experience soft rot is brought on in the spring just before bloom and again in the summer months as a result of an oversupply of water after plants have been kept dry. Consistent watering throughout the growing season has helped keep soft rot to a minimum in all but the worst affected cultivars.

Cure of soft rot is difficult and there are many suggestions as to chemical treatment of infected rhizomes. In general this is locking the stable door after the horse has bolted. Once soft rot is noticed the infected plant should be scraped dry and left to further dry out in the sun. Even more drastic care can be taken by lifting the plant, scraping dry and then replanting after it has dried out. This is usually unnecessary.

Infected plants are most often growing vigorously when the disease is noticed. Even though the parent rhizome can be lost there is usually sufficient increase to ensure the continuing propagation of the cultivar.

Lest these last few paragraphs deter prospective iris growers, let me re-state that as a general rule tall bearded iris are hardy, easy to grow and easy to grow well. They are less prone to disease and far more resilient than most plants. Normal care and maintenance will just about ensure trouble-free iris growing.

In the southern hemisphere iris are just about pest-free. Snails and slugs can wreak havoc in the iris patch, but they are easily controlled by persistent search-and-destroy tactics or by the use of chemical pesticides. Snails and slugs love to establish home in thick clumps of tall bearded iris which afford them safe refuge. They become a menace in the flowering season if they are allowed to survive as they will climb the foliage and bloom stalks to feed on the delicate buds and flowers. Once they have climbed a flowering stalk they rarely, if ever, descend and the whole flowering spike can be ruined. Care must be taken if chemicals are used to ensure that domestic pets are not poisoned.

Defender powder and pellets are less attractive to pets than Baysol but there is no antidote readily available; many pets are readily attracted to Baysol for which, however, there is an antidote.

There are numerous types of thrips which can be of nuisance value in spring when the flowers are formed. They are a menace in hot dry conditions but the most commonly encountered gladiolus thrip does little damage to the flowers although they may decimate the pollen, making hybridising difficult. Control is not easy and as most of the more effective insecticides cause a streaking effect on the flowers the cure is often worse than the complaint.

Control is aided by keeping the plants well watered and the author's approach is to do just that and accept the bad season with the good. It is interesting to note that with iris, just as with roses, the thrips prefer the lighter coloured cultivars to the darker. I can remember two successive seasons of the magnificent blue bearded pale blue iris 'Good Morning America'. In 1981 the flowers were thrip-infected and the iris was unpopular, few were sold and the clump became large. In 1982 thrip were virtually not seen, the iris was one of the most popular in the garden and was sold out early in the digging season.

Aphids are common in most gardens and although they inflict little direct harm some varieties are responsible for the transmission of virus. These pests are easily disposed of by the use of Malathion or Metasystox. Malathion is an effective contact spray and plants will need to be resprayed every 7 to 10 days, while Metasystox is sytemic and has a residual effect which lasts three weeks to a month.

Propagation

Propagation of tall bearded iris is achieved vegetatively by taking the increase or daughter plants from the mother rhizome. A sharp knife should be used to cut the young plants away and they should be leaf and root pruned as previously described. Plants so propagated will always be identical with the mother plant.

It is remarkable the number of people who believe that cultivars can 'just change' in the garden. A common feeling is that iris revert to other colours. More than once I have heard people lament that several years ago they purchased some differently coloured iris but they 'all reverted to the white one'. Colour and form 'sports', which are relatively common in camellias and roses, are extremely rare in iris. The usual answer to the above problem is that for some reason some of the less hardy iris plants have died while the strongest and most vigorous iris (it is inevitably 'the white one') has flourished, increased and hence spread to take over the spot vacated by the now-dead coloured ones.

Landscaping with Iris

Many people like to grow their iris in a separate garden where their cultural needs can be attended to without interference from other plants, but TB iris can usually be planted in the general garden. There is much to be said for a great massed display of iris which burst into bloom simultaneously, pervading the October air with their perfume and dazzling the eye with their colour and form, but unfortunately there is a long wait till the next bloom season.

Landscaping with iris in the average garden is easy, and a beautiful effect can be obtained by underplanting trees with low to medium height shrubs, then planting iris with a mass of annuals in the foreground. To obtain the best effect the trees should be in bloom or showing nice foliage at iris time. A particularly lovely effect can be obtained by using the crab apple (*Malus floribunda hillieri*) or the flowering plums (*Prunus blieriana* or *P. nigra*) underplanted with rugosa roses, tall bearded iris and annuals. The trees, roses and iris enjoy similar conditions and while the bloom of the plums would be finished by mid-October their beautiful foliage would be in evidence. The crab apple and roses flower with the iris and are beautiful throughout the year. Other lovely crab apples are *Malus ioensis* and the dark pink *M. ioensis rubra*.

Early flowering tall bearded iris are complemented by many other spring flowering shrubs and trees and are also effective in a massed planting of bulbs.

There are also mid-season and late bloomers which extend the flowering season from mid-September right through into November and often into December. The flowering season is correspondingly earlier in warmer climates and later in cooler climates while climatic conditions throughout the whole growing season will have an effect on bloom time in any particular year. Some hybridisers (the author included) are working on extending the flower season by producing earlier or later blooms, while others are producing remontant plants, that is, plants that rebloom in either summer, autumn or winter. Much is to be gained by producing plants that can give a second period of bloom but, unfortunately, many of the rebloomers flower when the plant is in a semi-dormant or dormant period of growth and although the flowers are welcome and most beautiful they are often not complemented by strong, attractive foliage. Late bloomers extend the season but the problem here is that warmer temperatures reduce the life of each individual flower; extreme heat can often result in burnt-up flowers after one day. The development of early bloom is of particular interest to gardeners in frost-free climates. Early growth and early bloom produce individual flowers that last longer than the normal three days and produce flowers in a garden setting alive with the early spring annuals, bulbs and flowering trees and shrubs.

Flowering Spike

The choice of a background and foreground for TB iris is closely related to the height of the flowering spike. Figure 4 indicated that the normal range for these spikes is 70–100cm.

Just as there are desirable traits in plant habit there are also desirable traits in the flower spike:

1. *Strength*—the spike should be strong, able to support the flowers and sufficiently rigid to ensure that it will not be blown over by the wind. A good iris should not need staking in the garden.

2. *Proportion*—the spike should be in proportion to the foliage. It should be tall enough for the flowers to be above the foliage. Further, the branches that make up the spike should be evenly spaced down the spike.

3. *Presentation*—the spikes should be well branched with each branch able to display the blooms gracefully and uncluttered. Each branch should have multiple buds to ensure a long flowering period—a minimum of 3 branches and 6 blooms. Some iris are equally satisfactory if they carry fewer buds to the spike but multiple spikes to the rhizome. An example of the latter is the beautiful light pink iris 'Vanity'. This classic beauty, a great garden favourite of mine, often has only 4 buds to the spike but will at times send up 3 or more spikes from a single rhizome.

The concurrence of open flowers on the various branches of the spike is also important. A flower from each branch may open simultaneously, making a great splash of colour and giving an ideal spike for showing. Alternatively, the flowers may open intermittently, giving a longer period of bloom in the garden.

It can be amazing how quickly the flowering spikes emerge from the foliage. A guide, although not foolproof, for telling if a plant is to flower is a noticeable curving of the central leaves in the fan of foliage. The presence of a spike can be confirmed by gently feeling the base of the fan.

In the early stages of development the spike can be brittle and care should be taken to avoid knocking the spikes, especially when weeding. It is thus advisable to have your iris clumps weed-free prior to the flowering season.

After reaching full height the rapid change in the appearance of the spike slows down. The flowers now develop in size. The time taken from the emergence of the spike to the start of flowering varies considerably but can be less than two weeks.

The Flower

Those characteristics of the individual TB iris bloom considered desirable have evolved over time. This is not uncommon with plants which are under the eye of an active group of hybridisers. The major aim of the modern hybridisers has been improving the quality of the individual bloom in form, substance and colour. The basic structure of the flower is shown in Figure 8.

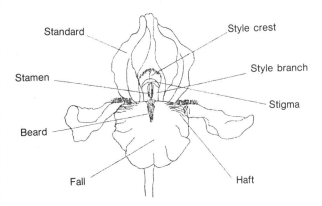

Fig. 8 The structure of the iris flower

Form is determined by the balance between the standards and the falls, neither being unnecessarily large compared with the other. The standards should be closed or touching, held erect yet nicely curved at the top; the falls should flare or semi-flare, be wide at the haft and held firmly in position. These attributes are enhanced by a flower with good firm substance, a property which ensures that the flower will stand up to the weather and keep well. Ruffling and fluting enhance the appearance of the flower while lacing of the petal edges can be another attraction. Colour in itself is a personal choice but in general the colour should be clear and bright. Bicolours and plicatas should have clarity and precision either in contrast or blending of the colour patterns. Although the purists do not like heavy striations of a different colour in the haft area, this can be most pleasing in some varieties. Fragrance is another added virtue and most cultivars have some fragrance, ranging in intensity from light to very heavy. The tall bearded iris fragrance is sweet and can be overpowering. Most people find it pleasant.

Several of the individual colours and colour patterns in the tall bearded iris can be grouped together. Remember that in each colour pattern there are many, many iris and hybridisers are increasing the number annually. The only colour not found in TBs so far is a fire engine red (and hybridisers are working on that). Flowers whose colour is the same in both standards and falls are referred to as *selfs* or *self-coloured*.

Whites

A stock joke among irisarians is the novice grower who announces proudly, 'I have *the* white one', yet it is amazing the number of people who come to the nursery and make that exact statement. Most are happy to learn that there are cool whites, warm whites, creamy whites, blue whites, that the form and substance and branching vary from one variety to another, that they flower early, mid-season and late, that some rebloom and that they come adorned with a variety of coloured beards, be they white, yellow, blue tipped yellow, blue, orange, tangerine or red, but there are still those sceptics who think you are 'putting one over' them or that the beards are painted on or dyed or other such monstrous things because they *know* 'there is only one white iris'.

Most white iris come from intercrossing two whites or a white and a blue but some come from the yellow-pink breeding line. This is particularly true of the red bearded whites.

It is interesting to note that I now grow very few of the iris that I grew and cherished ten years ago. Such is the improvement being made in tall bearded iris that only the great iris stand the test of time. In giving a list of recommendations I have tried to select only those that I consider will still be grown proudly ten years hence.

'**Wedding Vow**' How many superlatives can you record? Colour is often very pure white, sometimes with a blue influence. It is certainly in the cool white colour range with a basically white-tipped yellow beard. Plant habit, growth and disease resistance are all excellent. Flower form and bud placement are outstanding, making this an excellent garden and show bench variety. 'Wedding Vow' flowers early to mid season and continues to bloom through till late in the season. **Plate 7.**

'**White Lightning**' This is another strong and vigorous grower with all good garden qualities. The flower is pure white with a yellow haft influence and strong yellow beards. 'White Lightning' flowers very early in the season and continues well into mid-season. It is bred from yellow lines and is an excellent parent, producing yellows, pinks and mauves as well as whites when used for breeding with suitable iris. It was combined with the apricot 'Georgie Girl' to produce my beautiful yellow iris 'Joan McClemens'. **Plate 9.**

'**Leda's Lover**' is just about the ultimate for perfection of form; rounded, ruffled and fluted pure white petals make a lovely flower. **Plate 10.**

'**Rellie**' flowers early in the season, has an orange-red beard and grows vigorously. A good parent when used with suitable iris. **Plate 11.**

'**Bubbly Mood**' is a large, quality, ruffled white.

'**Chapeau Blanc**' is difficult to classify. It is a blue-white with pale lemon beards tipped blue.

'**Cloud Fire**' is a ruffled white with red beards.

'**Crystalyn**' is a large ruffled blue-white with white beards. Great quality. **Plate 12.**

'**Heart Mountain**' is a white with tangerine-red beards.

'**Jolimont**' is a quality clear white Australasian Dykes Medal winner, bred by John Baldwin. Great show branching and excellent growth habits.

'**Cascade Pass**' is a strong-growing white-bearded white that is worth special mention because it has a quality flower and is a reliable rebloomer. It will regularly produce a mass of bloom throughout May, June and July even into August.

'**Ice Sculpture**' is a new iris which opens ice blue and quickly turns white. It has huge imposing flowers, is well branched and a good grower.

'**Toasted Almond**' is a vigorous almond-white to pale ecru of exquisite form with ruffles galore. It is a new iris from Joe Ghio in the United States. **Plate 13.**

'**Heaven Helped**' is a classic white with pinkish beards.

'**Skating Party**' is a very large pure white. One of the best.

'**White Elephant**' is a huge white with lemon beard.

'**Memorandum**' Well branched, late blooming, clear white.

'**America's Cup**' is a strong, clean white.

Blues

True spectrum blue is a difficult colour to obtain in the plant kingdom and most of the blue iris available have some violet in them. Breeding for blues usually involves the crossing of blues or crossing a blue with a white. In the blue class there is a great range of colour, from the very pale blues right through to rich, dark cobalt blues. Here, as in the whites, there are a lot of excellent iris.

'**Flair**' is a pale blue of excellent garden habits. The flowers are large, nicely formed, ruffled and well placed on the strong spikes. This iris flowers mid-season and is top quality. It has rebloomed for us in July.

'**Good Morning America**' is another pale blue but the soft colour is lit up with strong electric-blue beards giving a beautiful effect. This iris flowers early to mid-season and is a highlight in the garden.

'**Divine Duchess**' is a superb soft silvery-blue with white beards. **Plate 14.**

'**Vivien**' is the best of the red-bearded blues. It is a clean clear colour on a plant with good garden qualities.

'**Autograph**' is pale blue with dark navy-blue beards.

'**Breakers**' is an outstanding rich mid-blue. Often reblooms.

'**Chico Maid**' is a late flowering light blue with deep-blue beards.

'**Sweetwater**' is an early flowering light sky blue with very big flowers on strong spikes. It grows very strongly but is slow to increase.

'**Sapphire Hills**' is probably the purest shade of blue. Again it is a good grower with rapid increase. Spikes are well formed and the flower is nicely shaped although a little narrow at the haft.

'**Full Tide**' has long been a top favourite and will remain so. This very vigorous and floriferous iris has admirable garden qualities. The flower is flared and ruffled and often has a silver margin to the mid-blue petals. This is a great iris. It flowers throughout the early and mid-season and often reblooms in winter. **Plate 15.**

'**Altruist**' is a soft, light blue with some white. Outstanding.

'**High Waters**' is a very vigorous mid to dark blue.

'**Just Magic**' is an icy blue with white beards.

'**Honkytonk Blues**' is an unusual blue washed over white. A superb iris and very different. **Plate 16.**

'**Admiralty**' is the darkest of the quality blues available and one of the quickest increasers around. Flower spikes are short and there are not a lot of buds per spike but the flowers are well formed and the bloom prolific. This iris is one of the first to bloom in the season.

'**Loyal Devotion**' is a clean light blue.

'**Music Maestro**' is a mid- to dark-blue.

'**Navy Waves**' is a navy-blue of excellent garden habits.

'**Pacific Grove**' is a huge mid-blue.

'**Penchant**' is an award-winning light- to mid-blue.

'**Silverado**' is a cool, silvery, light blue of outstanding form and excellent growth. Wonderful. **Plate 17.**

'**Victoria Falls**' is a mid to dark blue, very large and extravagantly ruffled and fluted. It is characterised by a white blaze beneath the beard, is a very strong and vigorous grower which flowers mid-season to late and has a tendency to rebloom.

'**Scandia Delight**' is a super quality sky-blue.

'**Rapture in Blue**' is another quality mid-sky-blue.

'**Song of Norway**' is a pale-blue with a darker blue beard.

'**Tide Crest**' is a hyacinth-blue with darker hafts.

'**Wind Surfer**' is a tall light blue with a white blaze.

'**Pledge Allegiance**' is a mid-dark blue with self beards.

'**Sky Echo**' is a nice icy blue with lighter falls.

'**Blue Glory**' is a sky-blue.

'**Caribbean Dream**' is a well formed mid-blue.

'**Fort Bragg**' is a multibudded light blue bitone.

'**G'day Mate**' is a mid- to dark-blue with a delightful perfume.

'**Scented Nutmeg**' is a mid-dark blue with nutmeg fragrance.

Purples

Great advances in the purple colouration have been made in recent years. Hybridisers have given this regal colour the attention it deserves and an excellent selection of purple iris is available.

'Dusky Challenger' is a very dark black-purple of outstanding form. Needs cold winters to thrive. **Plate 18.**

'His Lordship' is a blue-purple.

'Holy Night' is a very dark purple. Marvellous growth and vigour.

'Noble House' is a deep blue-purple. Tall majestic spikes.

'Barry Gaulter' is a super quality, huge dark purple.

'Lord Olivier' is a purple with texture veining, which adds distinction. **Plate 19.**

'Royal Kingdom' is a red-purple with dark blue beards.

'Titan's Glory' is a royal purple of excellent form, vigour and growth.

'Gyro' is a huge bright purple, multibudded.

'Velvet Vista' is a beautiful, ruffled, early blooming purple iris raised in Australia by John Baldwin. This prolific bloomer has the added advantage of rebloom and is an Award of Merit winner.

'Neil Diamond' is a dark violet-purple of good form.

'Think Big' is a very large, dark purple.

Blacks

Development of black iris has been slow and there are few quality iris in this colour range. Dark iris are developed from both the blue-purple side and the red side. Many flower late in the season, being burned up by the hot sun, so flower substance is of paramount importance.

'Black Dragon' is very dark, good form, moderate branching.

'Blackout' is really black. Tall and vigorous.

'Darkside' is black-purple with black beards. Ruffled.

'Houdini' is ruffled, well branched and very dark. **Plate 20.**

'Interpol' is one of the more reliable blacks. It has a mustard-tipped beard, grows vigorously and is of good form. It is a very late bloomer. **Plate 21.**

'Navy Chant' is a blue-black.

'Night Ruler' has medium-sized, ruffled black flowers.

'Raven Hill' is very dark purple, near black.

'Bordello' is a smooth dark red-purple black that flowers early. **Plate 22.**

'Witches Sabbath' is a dark purple, near black with bronze-yellow beards. Show spikes. **Plate 23.**

'Before the Storm' is the blackest yet.

'Black Fantasy' is maroon-black.

'Satin Satan' is dark purple-black.

Pale Blue-Purples

There is another group of iris in that elusive colour range between blues and purple. This includes lavenders, mauves, lilacs, light violets, heliotropes and blue orchid colours.

'Mary Frances' is a difficult iris to describe. Perhaps blue lavender or blue mauve fit it best for colour but there are not enough superlatives to describe the plant. Easy growing, vigorous and healthy plants produce beautiful spikes adorned by the well spaced ruffled blooms. This is a top award winner that does well everywhere and has universal appeal. **Plates 24,25.**

'Orchidarium' is a new iris from the United States and is a sensation. It is in the same blue-lilac tones as its parent 'Mary Frances' but is improved in form. This iris is destined to be a top favourite. **Plate 26.**

'Dusky Jewel' is a raspberry-violet.

'Extravagant' is an amethyst-violet.

'Fifth Dimension' has rum-violet standards with lavender falls rimmed plum-violet.

'Rondetta' is in the rosy orchid with a blue influence colour range. Growth habits are good, flower quality and spike are superb and the blooms are accented by tangerine beards. **Plate 27.**

'**Breakfast at Tiffanys**' is a mulberry-violet.

'**Crystal Cathedral**' is a pale lavender, near white.

'**Gauguin**' is a mulberry red-violet.

'**Sugartime**' is a lavender-orchid.

'**Taffeta Bow**' is a rosy orchid. **Plate 28.**

'**Taj Regis**' is a lavender with brown hafts.

'**Persian Berry**' is a fancy raspberry to dark rosy orchid with darker hafts. It is a most attractive and unusual flower of good form on a plant with all good habits. It flowers mid-season. **Plate 29.**

Reds

Having looked at one side of the spectrum let us turn our attention to the other end. Pure pillar-box red is still a dream in tall bearded iris, just as blue is proving elusive in rose breeding. Perhaps the genes are just not there but great advances have been made in recent years. To the forefront at the moment is Joe Ghio's magnificent new 'red' iris 'Lady Friend'. Most iris in the red range have lacked form or vigour, have flowered very late and have been on poor spikes. Joe Ghio combined his brown line with tangerine-bearded yellows to produce this unique iris. It is in advance of the advanced and opens up a whole new possibility in breeding lines. No doubt it will be expensive and remain so for some time but will be well worth the asking price.

'**Lady Friend**' is tall, imposing, extremely vigorous and very early. The form and branching are good and the colour is unique. This colour is a rich garnet-rose-red with tangerine-red beards. Ruffled petals, large and wide, complete the picture of this iris which will be an all time favourite. **Plate 30.**

'**Burgundy Bubbles**' is a ruffled burgundy-red.

'**Be a Devil**' has ruby-red standards, darker falls and bronze beards.

'**Friday Night**' is a brown-red.

'**Marauder**' is a maroon-red with gold beards.

'**Burgundy Cherry**', also from Joe Ghio, is a ruffled true burgundy colour. It is late flowering, impressive in form and of good garden habits.

'**Mulled Wine**' is a raspberry-burgundy.

'**Warrior King**' is a dark brown-red with a glossy sheen.

'**Rubistar**' is a rich, ruby red.

Browns

Now that a quality red has arrived from the Ghio brown line it is fitting to discuss the browns where again progress was very slow until the master hybridiser turned his attention to this area. His success was achieved by using 'New Moon' and 'Denver Mint' derivatives with his outstanding breeding iris 'Ponderosa'. 'Ponderosa' has the ability to pass on form, vigour and branching while being recessive for colour. This property it has passed on to its outstanding child 'Entourage'. These have been two great parents. In recommending brown iris we find mainly iris bred by Joe Ghio.

'**Flare Up**' is probably the best all round brown available. Branching is superb, colour is light mid-brown and growing habits and flowering are all excellent. I have had a spike of 'Flare Up' with six flowers open simultaneously. **Plate 31.**

'**Bright Warrior**' has golden-brown standards, darker falls.

'**Brassy Broad**' is a brassy gold.

'**Cable Car**' is a large mid-brown.

'**Cafe Society**' is a honey-tan.

'**Ginger Swirl**' has tan standards and rim, and orchid falls.

'**Swain**' is a super quality brown bitone. **Plate 32.**

'**Veneer**' could be the nicest of all the Ghio browns. It is a rich deep brown with lovely form and superior branching.

'Indian Territory' is a well formed mid-season bloomer in a red-brown colour. It is tall, well branched and strong of growth and increase.

'Brimstone' is a bright brown of good vigour. It flowers early in the season, multiplies quickly and makes a good flowering display. Form is average.

'Rustler' is a super quality brown bitone. **Plate 33.**

'Praline' is a bronze-toned brown.

'Rancho Grande' is a rosy-tan and honey-tan bitone.

'Sugar Daddy' is a caramel-brown with a violet flush.

'Los Banos' is a rich light brown.

Oranges

Orange iris have been few and the quality has not been good until recently. Now great improvements have been made and some really nice things are available. Breeding of orange iris is closely related to pinks and tangerine-bearded yellows. Closely related to the orange iris are the melon and apricot tones and these will be discussed together.

'Bogota' is a super quality dark orange.

'Orange Celebrity' Brilliant orange, red beards.

'Close Your Eyes' is a creamy melon-apricot.

'First Movement' Outstanding rich apricot. **Cover.**

'Cinderella's Coach' is a pumpkin-orange.

'Deft Touch' is a peachy apricot.

'Edna's Wish' is a salmon-orange.

'Fame' is a brilliant yellow-orange.

'Furnace Creek' is a rich orange with red beards.

'Hindenberg' is a clear, bright orange.

'Oktoberfest' is a rich mid-orange.

'Imagine Me' is an apricot bitone.

'Malaguena' is a well-formed orange with some pink.

'Montevideo' is a tall, late flowering, clear orange.

'Santiago' is a heavily ruffled dark orange with red beards.

'Mandolin' would be one of my first iris planted in any collection. It is a rich musk-melon to orange-sherbert colour. The flowers are large, beautifully formed and ruffled. Growth is prolific and 'Mandolin' flowers very early in the season. **Plate 34.**

'Orchard Girl' is a clear orange with red beards.

'Nivea' is an unusual burnt orange.

'Metaphor' is an apricot-cream blended with peach and coral beards. This iris is an excellent grower and the mid-season blooms are of very good form. **Plate 35.**

'Samurai Silk' is a creamy orange-apricot.

'Sneak Preview' is a clear apricot.

'Preface' is an early flowering coral-peach-apricot of good form and heavy substance. This iris can rebloom and has all good qualities. **Plate 36.**

Pinks

The pink iris are related in their development to the yellows and oranges and here the advancement in recent years has been outstanding. There are now many, many good pinks in a full range of tones from the palest of flesh colours to a dark, rich rose-pink. Much of the development of recent quality pinks has been a result of hybridising of Nate Rudolph and Joe Gatty in the US and their lines of breeding trace back to Fay and Hall iris of the 1940s and 1950s. Hybridising good pinks is now a relatively easy process. Some nice things are obtained from Ghio's 'Entourage', Gatty's 'White Lightning' and its pink derivatives, Rudolph's 'Pink Angel', 'Lemon Mist' and their derivatives. 'Mandolin', 'Metaphor' and 'Georgia Girl' have all proven good parents in the apricot, melon, peach tonings already mentioned so there are unlimited opportunities in this colour range.

'Pink Taffeta' is a starting point for a modern collection of pink iris. This top award winner is tall, vigorous and well formed. Colour is a clear light pink with a red beard. **Plate 37.**

'Anna Belle Babson' is a deep but bright pink. Late flowering.

'Bubble Up' is a heavily-ruffled mauve-pink. Lovely.

'Cameo Wine' is a pink bitone.

'Carved Cameo' is a creamy peach-pink. Late flowering.

'Con Amore' is a lovely ruffled light pink.

'Dance Music' is a full ruffled light pink with a rose infusion.

'Designer Gown' is a variable light- to mid-pink with a grape infusion.

'Exhilaration' is a ruffled and laced salmon-pink.

'Vanity' is a mid-season to late iris of clear light pink. Growth and increase are both excellent. Spikes are sometimes short of buds but this is compensated for by the number of bloom stalks. A great iris. **Plate 38.**

'Entourage' is a dusky rose-pink from another line of breeding. Again all the top qualities are there. Another great iris.

'Frosty Jewels' is a ruffled mid-pink.

'Pink Belle' is a ruffled mid-pink with a tangerine beard. **Plate 39.**

'Goddess' is a soft peach-pink. **Plate 40.**

'Mollie Savell' is a peach-pink with an apricot infusion. **Plate 41.**

'Helen Ruth' is a baby-ribbon pink.

'Melissa Sue' is a laced mid-pink.

'Miss Jeannie' is a dark mid-pink with a slight bitone effect.

'Mittagong' is a soft creamy pink.

'Soprano' is a pink bitone.

'Natural Beauty' is a lovely soft, ruffled, light pink.

'Prejudice' is a short growing, mid-pink. **Plate 42.**

'Beverly Sill' is a well-formed, rounded, coral-pink. Flowers are ruffled and laced and growth is vigorous. This iris blooms late.

'Highness' is a texture veined, hot pink with heavy substance, good growth and flower habits.

'Peach Lustre' is a tall peach-pink.

'Pink Swan' is a ruffled mid-pink with a hint of blue.

'Tiffany Time' is a ruffled and laced light pink.

'Pacific Peach' is an early flowering buff-peach-pink with a persimmon beard. It is strong and very vigorous, in fact increase is prolific.

'Pink Jamboree' is a rhodamine-pink with a brick-red beard.

Yellows

Yellow is a dominant colour in tall bearded iris and there are many good quality yellows available. They vary in colour from pale lemon to intense gold. Breeding of yellows has not been dominated by any particular hybridiser although both Rudolph and Gatty have a superior line going in the light to mid-yellows. The breeding of yellows is often related to pink breeding and the recessive red-bearded whites. Many of the quality yellow iris available trace back to 'Denver Mint' and more recently to 'New Moon' and its derivatives.

'New Moon' is in itself a good iris and a great parent. It can be prone to rot and even though the flower has good substance it is not long lasting. With these faults overlooked we have a large flower of near perfect form and lovely clear yellow colour. Branching is variable but growth is good. **Plate 43.**

'Lemon Mist' remains the best of the Rudolph yellows for all round performance. This clear lemon-yellow is a large beautifully formed flower on spikes which are often on the short side. Branching is good and both growth and increase are excellent. 'Lemon Mist' flowers for a long period from mid-season.

'Bahloo' is a rich yellow. Excellent growth.

'Catalyst' is a short golden-yellow. Multibudded.

'Opportunity' is a super quality, rich golden yellow.

'Classico' is a quality cream.

'Dance Man' is a huge bright yellow.

'Gold Country' is a large gold of excellent form and growth. **Plate 44.**

'Solano' is a very early large rich golden-yellow. It is a quality iris of good form, excellent growth and increase and branching to support the many buds and give a long bloom season.

'Simply Pretty' is a light lemon-yellow.

'Preferred Stock' is a rich golden yellow.

'Sunny Delight' is bred from 'Solano' and 'Luscious Lemon'. Its colour is somewhere between the two and it combines the good qualities of both. This superior clear yellow flowers mid-season for a long period.

'Fission' is a well-formed yellow bitone.

'Flaming Victory' is yellow with red beards. Lovely.

'Lightning Bug' is a soft creamy yellow.

'Lemon Lyric' is somewhat of a bitone. Standards are lemon, falls are cream edged lemon with lemon beards. It is laced, fluted and ruffled. This new iris is absolutely beautiful and its good growth indicates it could be one of the great iris.

'Joan McClemens' is another new iris bred by the author. It flowers very early on extremely strong and quick increasing plants. The form is particularly beautiful and this iris is destined to be one of the best yellows. **Plate 45.**

'Temple Gold' flowers mid-season to late. It is a tall ruffled and laced bright yellow of perfect form on excellent show spikes. One of the best. **Plate 46.**

'Black Hills Gold' Yellow bitone, pink infusion.

'Yukon Delight' is a rich golden yellow.

'Radiant Energy' is a heavily ruffled, rich glowing yellow. **Plate 47.**

Then there are those iris which combine yellow and white without being in the amoena pattern of white standards and yellow falls. In this bracket there are six iris, all individually distinct and all worth a place in the garden.

'Launching Pad' has been around now for a few years. The rather short, well branched spikes come into flower early in the season. Growth and increase are good. The flowers have yellow standards, white middle of falls edged yellow with orange-yellow beards.

'Cream D'or' has lemon standards, flushed white, and white falls banded yellow.

'Treasure City' flowers mid-season to late and has simply huge blooms in the same colour pattern but with more of a lemon yellow.

'Joyce Terry' is in the same colour pattern as 'Launching Pad' but is taller, more clear in the colour contrast and flowers mid-season. **Plate 48.**

'Liqueur Creme' has creamy white standards and white falls edged yellow.

'Light Beam' has lemon standards and white falls stitched lemon.

'Love the Sun' is a yellow bitone.

Greens

Then there are the 'green' iris. While there is no pure leaf-green iris some iris do give a very green effect, either from the white side or the yellow side.

'Green and Gifted' is a creamy green with a pastel overlay and brown beards.

'Forbidden' is a ruffled greenish-blue.

'Evening Mist' is a soft, creamy green with a milk-violet wash.

'Hello Hobo' has lemon-green standards and brown-tan falls.

'Irish Spring' is a warm white with a distinct green influence. Flower form is very wide and ruffled. Blooms are late and held on very strong spikes. Growth and increase are prolific.

'Song of Erin' is probably the best all round green iris available but it is a pity that the spikes often blow over in the weather and really need staking to be best appreciated. Colour is a chartreuse shade, bloom is early and continuous throughout the season. Branching is excellent to carry the numerous buds and increase is prolific. **Plate 49.**

Plicatas

Although the plicata pattern is anything but new—plicatas have been grown for as long as iris have—many startling advances have been made in recent years to make this a particularly popular pattern. Basically a plicata is an iris with a ground colour stitched, dotted and/or edged in another colour. Recent developments have seen a fusion of colours in the base of some irises and others with the standards edged a different colour to that of the falls.

New colour combinations showing up mainly in the breeding lines of Keith Keppel and Jim Gibson, both from California, make the plicata pattern an exciting one to work with as a hybridiser and also a great one to grow and enjoy.

Plicatas are, in general, recessive so to obtain them, plicatas need to be crossed with plicatas or with iris having plicatas in their background. Of all the tall bearded iris they set seed most readily and germinate most readily. This is an ideal pattern for the beginner to work with as results are easy to obtain and colour variation in the resultant seedlings is often great.

There are many plicatas of outstanding quality available and each year more beauties come on to the market. Many of the plicatas are in the blue on white or purple on white pattern, that is, a ground colour of white with petals margined in blue or purple. The outstanding iris in this pattern has been 'Stepping Out', for many years top of the American Iris Society popularity poll, and an iris that figures in the parentage of many top quality plicatas. Unfortunately 'Stepping Out', for all its universal appeal, has never grown well or flowered well for me nor for that matter anyone in the Sydney area.

'Beguine' has salmon-apricot standards suffused rose-pink and apricot falls dotted rose-pink.

'Chuckles' is a salmon-pink to apricot stitched and edged rose-pink.

'Daredevil' is a white-edged blue with red beards.

'Date Bait' has light pink standards and white falls stitched pink.

'Eagles Flight' has a white ground with rosy-violet stitching on standards and darker stitching on falls.

'Rococo Valley' is an outstanding Australian raised iris. Alan Johnson of Tongala crossed 'Rococo' with the blue-violet blazed white 'Utah Valley' to obtain 'Rococo Valley', an iris which has set the standard for Australian raised varieties for many years. This white ground stitched light to mid blue iris flowers early and continues through most of the season due to its huge bud count. I have regularly found spikes with 3 or more buds in each socket and a total of 15 or 16 flowers on a spike is quite common. Furthermore the spikes carry the blooms in perfect position, making this a great show iris, often having 3 or 4 flowers open simultaneously. 'Rococo Valley' grows well, increases rapidly and is disease free. Unfortunately it has not proven to be a parent—I have never been able to gather pollen or set a pod on it. **Plate 50.**

'Auric' has yellow standards and white falls edged rosy brown.

'Parquet' has subtle tones of rosewood and sandalwood.

'Picasso' has a white ground stitched dark blue-violet.

'Under a Cloud' is white with overall violet stitching.

'Palace Gossip' has a white ground edged burgundy-purple.

'Blue Ballet' has icy blue standards, white falls edged blue lavender with a paler outer rim.

'Blue Petticoats' is another Schreiner iris of about the same vintage as 'Rococo Valley'. It is from the 'Rococo' breeding line. Colour pattern is much the same but the blue is darker than on 'Rococo Valley'. 'Blue Petticoats' grows well and flowers early in the season. The blooms are heavily ruffled and fluted to the extent of appearing upturned. Branching is adequate.

'Going My Way' comes from Jim Gibson and is a great iris. Colour is a rich blue-purple edging on a clear white ground and the flower is of good size and exquisite form. Growth and branching are good as are all the plant qualities. 'Going My Way' flowers continuously from mid-season. **Plate 51.**

'Kiss' is another exquisite flower. Lavender-blue edging on white and great wide form create a garden spectacle. Spikes are short but the branching is good as are all the growth and increase habits. 'Kiss' flowers mid season. It is amusing to note how 'Kiss' was named. It was originally tagged as a seedling number K155 in the hybridiser's garden. A visitor misread the label and exclaimed, "Kiss, what a lovely name", and so an iris was named. **Plate 52.**

'Blue Staccato' is an early flowering tall and ruffled white ground plicata sharply edged with deep blue. This vigorous and prolific new plicata is destined for great popularity as all its garden habits are good. **Plate 53.**

'Charmed Circle' is an early flowering dark roslyn-blue on white plicata. Colour delineation is excellent and growth habits are top class. Spikes are on the short side but branching is excellent. This is a quality iris.

'Earl of Essex' is a reblooming white with light blue edging.

'Hot Streak' is a brilliant yellow with falls edged red. Startling.

'Circus Stripes' is a novelty. Flowers are medium sized and white with blue-purple vertical striping throughout. Growth is adequate, as is the branching and garden performance. Flowers are medium sized, a little long in the falls, and of average quality. **Plate 54.**

'Indiscreet' has salmon-cream falls edged magenta-purple. Near solid magenta standards.

'Kissing Circle' is a white-edged blue-violet.

'Purple Pepper' is white-edged, dotted and solidly peppered in purple.

'Gentle Rain' is also from Keith Keppel. This is an early flowering white ground plicata with mid-blue edging and dotting. Colour and form are superb, growth and increase are excellent. The spikes are often short with branching a little low to the ground.

'Romanticist' has peach-pink standards, suffused mauve. Cream-buff falls are flushed pink with rosy mauve hafts and edges.

'Rondo' flowers mid-season to late. The blooms are large and well formed with a clear white base and rosy-violet plicata edging. All garden qualities are good.

'Sterling Stitched' is a white-edged blue with light red beards.

'Closed Circuit' is a white-edged purple.

'Raspberry Fudge' has raspberry-tan standards and cream falls with dark raspberry-brown hafts and border. **Plate 55.**

'Rosarita' has buff standards, edged orchid rose, apricot-cream falls with a white centre and brown-rose hafts and edge.

'Polar Seas' Blue standards, white falls edged in violet.

'Jesse's Song' has a white ground with a light violet edging. Superb flower and an easy grower. Top award winner. **Plate 56.**

'Plum Gleam' is a Gibson iris of great form and vigour. Increase is quick. The large flowers on well branched stems are basically cream with smoky plum-taupe edging. **Plate 57.**

'Smoke Rings' is another Gibson iris, very vigorous and very quick of increase. It flowers mid-season and the colour is somewhat subdued, being lighter than 'Plum Gleam'. Again the base is cream with a light mauve dotting and edging. **Plate 58.**

'Alan Johnson' is a fancy white ground plicata with the standards heavily dotted and dashed in light blue and the falls pencil-lined in blue-violet. This vigorous and prolific iris was bred by the author and named after a famous Australian irisarian and hybridiser. It is an award of merit winner and also winner of the Gordon Loveridge Hybridisers' Medallion. **Plate 59.**

'Armada' has lavender-white standards and white falls banded dark violet-blue. **Plate 60.**

'Secret Melody' has an apricot ground, stitched raspberry. **Plate 61.**

'Snowbrook' is a pure white with a blue rim on the falls only. **Plate 62.**

'Asha Michelle' has soft yellow standards and white falls stitched in rose-brown with yellow beards. The flowers are ruffled and growth is good. **Plate 63.**

'Rare Treat' has a white ground precisely edged rich mid-blue. **Plate 64.**

The other plicatas worthy of mention are the exciting Keppel variegata plicatas 'Caramba' and 'Flamenco'. Both have yellow toned standards and fancy brown, yellow and white falls. Both are different and exciting with great form and tremendous colour. Unfortunately they have proved erratic in garden performance to this date. If and when they settle down they will be worthy additions to the garden.

Bicolours

Finally there is that large group of iris which can loosely be described as bicolours. These iris have standards of a colour different to that of the falls. Bitones have standards and falls of the same colour but different tones. Other specific terms used to describe these iris are *amoena*—white standards and differently coloured falls; *neglecta*—light blue standards, darker falls; *variegata*—yellow standards and darker falls; *reverse amoena*—darker coloured standards over white falls.

Neglectas

The neglecta pattern is very popular—and justifiably so. Progress has been rapid in recent years and there are many excellent neglectas available. In fact Joe Ghio's 'Mystique' would have to be the most popular iris released in the 1970s. Neglectas can be bred by intercrossing neglectas, crossing a neglecta to a self colour (usually in the blue range) or by crossing neglectas to amoenas. Others do turn up in bicolour breeding.

'**Blues Brothers**' has light blue standards and mid-blue falls. **Plate 65.**

'**Mystique**' flowers mid-season to late. The large ruffled flowers on well branched spikes have blue standards and rich blue-purple falls with the falls colour bleeding up into the midrib of the standards. Growth is good and the form is superb. This is a great iris. **Plate 66.**

'**Shadow Magic**' loses little by comparison with 'Mystique'. Basic colouring is similar but with 'Shadow Magic' there is a blue rim to the falls. Increase is very rapid and bloom is prolific. Spikes are a little on the short side.

'**Lady Vera**', bred by the author, is another well formed neglecta that blooms very early in the season. This extremely vigorous and quick increasing iris is often in full bloom before the end of August in Sydney and still in bloom at the end of October. It is very useful in landscaping with spring bulbs and annuals because of its early and continuous bloom. Branching is magnificent with 15 or more flowers to the stem being rather common.

'**Congratulations**' has rich blue standards and pansy-violet falls.

'**Nordic Seas**' has blue standards and dark violet falls.

'**Best Bet**' has blue standards and blue-purple falls.

'**In Town**' has blue standards, purple falls edged avender-blue and tangerine-red beards.

'**Physique**' has light blue standards, iridescent violet falls and bright red beards. **Plate 67.**

'**Success Story**' has light blue standards, fuchsian violet falls and lemon beards.

'**Surf Lady**' has pale blue standards, lavender-blue falls and large lemon beards.

'**Witch's Wand**' has dark violet standards, darker, near black falls and tangerine-red beards.

'**Mystic Waters**' is a pale and mid-blue of impeccable form.

'**Proud Tradition**' has light blue standards and rich blue falls.

'**Revolution**' has pale blue standards, dark violet-blue falls, mid orange-red beards.

Amoenas

In his search for the elusive pink amoena (white standards, pink falls) Barry Blyth of Tempo Two Nursery in Victoria has become the world leader in bicolour breeding. Some few years back, Barry used 'Sunset Snows', a small-flowered white and pink iris of New Zealand's Jean Stevens, as the basis of a breeding campaign that has produced bicolours rivalling the quality of the self colours and plicatas. Although he is yet to produce *the* quality pink amoena Barry has given the world some outstanding introductions on the way.

Having started with an iris as small and narrow as 'Sunset Snows', Barry readily concedes that many of his earlier introductions were small-flowered and somewhat narrow, but line breeding and the use of quality outcrosses has improved the form considerably and the colour range is superb. An obvious spin-off is Barry's more recent involvement in the development of bicolour plicatas and here again he is producing beautiful irises.

'**Ruffled Ballet**' is an American raised iris of outstanding quality. Pure white standards and clear sky blue falls adorn a ruffled flower of beautiful form. Growth and increase are satisfactory, as is the branching. Two sister seedlings of 'Ruffled Ballet' have also been introduced and are available. These are 'Moody Blue' and 'Cherished Memory'. Each of these is a quality iris in the same colour pattern and is worthy of a place in any garden.

'**Alpine Journey**' has white standards with yellow falls and beards.

'**Amber Snow**' has white standards, apricot falls and red beards.

'**Bernice Roe**' has white standards and yellow falls.

'**Crimson Snow**' has white standards, flushed orchid. Falls are rose-red, edged white and flushed pink.

'**Echo de France**' has white standards and lemon yellow falls.

'**Floral Act**' has white standards, pale blue falls and tangerine beards. **Plate 68.**

'**Glistening Icicle**' has white standards, blue falls.

'**Neutron Dance**' has white standards and golden yellow falls.

'**Olympiad**' is a silvery blue-white with a darker flush. Standards are darker than falls.

'**Oriental Alabaster**' has creamy white standards, creamy apricot falls and tangerine beards.

'**Perfect Couple**' has blue standards and white falls with a blue cast.

'**Precious Moments**' has creamy white standards and white falls.

'**Premier Edition**' has white standards and blue falls.

'**Royal Crusader**' has white standards and blue falls.

'**Kentucky Skies**' has white tinted blue standards and sky blue falls.

'**Windsong West**' is a reverse bicoloured hazy blue.

Variegatas and Other Bicolours

'**All That Jazz**' has yellow standards and brown-red falls. **Plate 69.**

'**Bengal Tiger**' has yellow standards, and yellow falls veined red.

'**Berry Sherbert**' is a pink and violet-mauve bicolour.

'**Champagne Elegance**' has pale lavender pink standards and buff apricot falls.

'**Dazzling Gold**' is a golden-yellow with red veins on falls.

'**Supreme Sultan**' has tan-gold standards and mahogany-red falls.

'**Edith Wolford**' has yellow standards and violet-blue falls. **Plate 70.**

'**Eurythmic**' has pink buff standards, and lavender-magenta falls with plum-burgundy hafts.

'**Heather Blush**' is a soft pink and amethyst-violet blended bicolour.

'**Heather Cloud**' is a pink and violet bicolour.

'**Latin Lark**' has buff-pink standards, with ruby-red falls edged buff-pink. **Plate 71.**

'**Liaison**' has pink standards, purple falls, pink edge and starburst pattern around red beards.

'**Mountain Violet**' has pale violet standards flushed pink, darker violet falls and tangerine beards.

'**Planned Treasure**' has soft pink standards, white falls washed orchid-purple and banded dark purple, and red beards. **Plate 72.**

'**Sweet Musette**' has flamingo-pink standards and rose falls with tangerine beards.

'**Syncopation**' has tan-gold standards, violet falls, brown hafts and gold beards.

'**Fanfaron**' is a yellow with red veins and overlay on falls.

'**Glitz 'n' Glitter**' has yellow standards. The falls are yellow with purple edging and streaking.

'**San Jose**' has caramel-brown standards with the same brown colouring washed over the violet falls. Form is excellent with ruffles galore and the growth is very vigorous. **Plate 73.**

'**Cameo Wine**' is difficult to classify. It is a startling iris from Barry Blyth in shades of pink—actually a pink bitone. Form is good and so are all its garden habits. This will be a very popular iris. **Plate 74.**

2 Other Bearded Iris

Other bearded iris are generally classified according to height and bloom period.

Miniature Dwarf Bearded Iris

The earliest blooms of the season come from the miniature dwarf bearded iris. The spikes, which are up to 20cm high, are rarely branched, so that 1–2 flowers per spike is normal. This lack of buds is compensated by the large number of bloom spikes obtained. The miniature dwarfs flower from early September and produce a massed display rapidly but they do need a cold winter to bloom well. In more temperate climates they will grow and increase but flowering is spasmodic and not as spectacular. Some will refuse to bloom at all unless frost chilled in the winter.

These iris are more demanding in their culture than tall bearded iris. They require full sun and perfect drainage. Fertilising, watering and general culture are similar to tall bearded iris but the miniature dwarfs, because of their rapid increase, probably need dividing more often. When dividing established clumps or planting new stock, early planting is essential to obtain bloom the following season, and March is the latest month for plants to be moved.

The miniature dwarfs come in a wide colour range and have colour combinations not seen in other iris. They are delightful plants for rock gardens or borders in an open sunny position.

Standard Dwarf Bearded Iris

The spikes of standard dwarf bearded iris are from 20 to 38cm high and are usually branched, giving more flowers per spike than the miniatures. They flower later in the season than the miniatures, with the bloom period of early standard dwarfs overlapping the late miniature dwarfs. All cultural requirements are similar to those for miniature dwarfs.

Because of the difficulty in obtaining bloom, dwarf bearded iris are not recommended for coastal areas of New South Wales and Queensland and corresponding climatic areas in New Zealand. They do require winter cold with 4–6 weeks of frost a minimum. They are easy to grow where climatic conditions are to their liking.

'Bay Ruffles' Light blue.
'Blue Line' White, blue beard.
'Bright Vision' Apricot.
'Bunny Hop' White and light yellow.
'Cherry Doll' Cherry-red to black-red.
'Delicate Pink' Creamy pink.
'Eye Bright' Gold, red-ray pattern.
'Gingerbread Man' Brown with rich blue-purple beards.
'Hi Honey' Pink and tan.
'Hi Sailor' White, blue spot.
'Honey Wind' Tan, darker stippling.
'Jade Mist' Smoky blue-green.
'Jazzamatazz' Cream standards, ruby falls edged cream.
'Lemon Rings' Lemon, deeper spot.
'Michael Paul' Dark black-violet. **Plate 75.**
'Making Eyes' (Blyth) Cream-lemon standards, red-violet falls edged lemon, cream beards. **Plate 76.**
'Mister Roberts' Gold.
'Moocha' Maroon-brown standards, lemon falls.
'My Sheba' Peach-pink, stitched maroon.
'Real Coquette' (Blyth) Pale blue standards, chartreuse-lemon falls, lilac-blue beards.
'Nimble Toes' White, blue plicata, red beard.
'Pale Star' Pale blue.
'Raspberry Jam' Raspberry pink.
'Small Flash' Yellow standards, red-purple falls edged yellow.
'Smoky Imp' Smoky pink-violet.
'Tricks' Pink and cream.

'Wind Rose' Pink bitone.
'Winelight' Burgundy.
'Wizard of Id' Antique gold, flushed purple. **Plate 77.**
'Zounds' Blue lilac and olive tan.

Intermediate Bearded Iris

Intermediate for height and for blooming period are the intermediate bearded iris. They are obtained by intercrossing the tall bearded iris with the dwarfs and range in height from 40 to 70cm, while they flower after the dwarfs but before the tall beardeds. A good quality IB iris should have flowers in proportion to the spike and be well branched. They are easier to grow in warmer, more humid areas than the dwarfs and have a wide colour range. All cultural requirements are similar to those for dwarf bearded iris.

'Aurean' Golden yellow.
'Avanelle' White.
'Buttered Pecan' Yellow stitched brown.
'Crackles' White stitched violet.
'Daiquiri' Golden apricot.
'French Silk' Light blue bitone.
'Harlow Gold' Yellow.
'Hellcat' Blue and purple.
'Honey Glazed' Cream and caramel.
'Impulse' Yellow.
'Rare Edition' 45cm. Clear white ground edged mulberry-purple.
'Logo' Apricot stitched and marked purple.
'Merry Life' Rose and white plicata.
'Midas Plush' Gold.
'O'Cool' White, lavender crescents.
'Only Foolin'' Brassy gold.
'Philanderer' Tan and ruby red.
'Raspberry Acres' 45cm. White with raspberry plicata edging.
'Posh' Apricot, orange bitone.
'Rebel Yell' Antique gold.
'Revved Up' Gold, red plicata dots.
'Romp' Apricot bitone.
'Shooting Sparks' Blue-purple on white plicata.
'Shugar' Salmon-pink.
'Strawberry Love' Rose-pink.
'Strum' White, cream and yellow.
'Tchin Tchin' Peach pink.

'Triplet' Rose standards, yellow and mauve falls.
'Tyrolienne' Lemon-buff and violet-tan.
'Silent Strings' 40cm. Light blue with a white beard tipped yellow.
'Vasqua' Blue-lavender, rosy overlay.
'Zing Me' Lemon, white and brown. **Plate 78.**
'Sundown Red' was bred by Paul Blyth and is a quality intermediate bearded. Basic colour is burgundy-red throughout with the falls slightly darker than the standards. **Plate 79.**
'Zoning' Cream, rosy lavender stitching, gold edge.

Miniature Tall Bearded Iris

The miniature tall bearded irises are just what the name indicates—smaller versions of the tall beardeds. They have the same height range as the intermediate bearded iris but bloom later with a profusion of spikes carrying proportionately smaller blooms. The tendency in breeding is towards tailored blooms with flaring form. These iris make small, densely floriferous clumps.

Miniature tall bearded iris have not been popular in Australia and the author's only experience with them was disastrous. Most of the miniature tall beardeds are badly infected with virus and show it quite readily. A collection imported from the US several years ago was destroyed in total by the Department of Agriculture, quarantine section, before getting into the author's hands. There is a place for these iris in the garden and eventually they may become available and popular.

A few of the better known varieties are 'Kaleidoscope', 'Joseph's Coat', 'Bit of Afton' and 'Widget'. They require similar treatment in the garden to tall bearded iris, although they are somewhat less demanding in their requirements.

Border Bearded Iris

Border bearded iris are lower growing versions of tall bearded iris. They are from the same breeding, but being on shorter stems they should have size of flower proportional to the height of the spike. Because they are really short-talls they bloom at the same time as the tall bearded iris and have the same colour range and patterns. These iris should be given exactly the same treatment as tall bearded iris and are ideal for planting in the front of the iris display or in rock gardens or perennial borders. Bennet Jones of the American Iris Society in *The World of Irises* recommends geum, dianthus, violas, iberis, pyrethrum, columbine and campanulas as compatible perennials of appropriate size. Of course there is also a multitude of annuals which could be used with border bearded iris to give a spectacular display.

'Irene's Love' Yellow standards, violet falls with brown rim.

'Pink Bubbles' is a clear light pink. Vigorous and beautiful. **Plate 80.**

'Whoop 'Em Up' is a dazzling variegata in yellow and red.

'Ambling' Orchid-blue and champagne-pink.

'Am I Blue' is a light blue with blue beards.

'Loving Cup' Sky blue standards, white falls touched blue.

'Inner Circle' has light blue standards, darker falls. **Plate 81.**

'Elsedina' is a rich blue-purple heavily stitched and edged on pure white plicata. This early flowering beauty sets new standards of excellence. **Plate 82.**

'Brown Lasso' has brown standards, violet falls with a brown rim.

'Marmalade Skies' Apricot-orange with a pink tinge in the standards.

'Bimini' Pale blue-white, mauve hafts.

'Borderline' White and yellow.

'Classic Treasure' White, blue rim on falls.

'Curacao' Pink-buff standards, plum-violet falls edged lilac. **Plate 83.**

'Soft Spoken' Lilac.

'Something Special' Flamingo pink.

'Eye Magic' grows to 45 cm and has gold standards, and gold falls with a red thumbprint. **Plate 84.**

Arils and Arilbreds

The pure aril irises are characterised by an aril or collar, usually white in colour, on one end of the seed, while the arilbreds are hybrids obtained by crossing the pure aril species with other bearded irises, usually tall bearded. Of the aril species the more common belong to the *Oncocyclus* and *Regelia* groups.

Oncocyclus Iris

Oncocyclus iris are natives of the Middle East, reaching north into Russia and south to the Mediterranean, where they grow mainly in arid areas without any summer rain. They normally bloom early in the spring, go dormant during summer and recommence growth in the autumn. Any summer moisture is likely to cause rhizome rot, although the plants need moisture in the growing season. They obviously need special care to be grown successfully and to many people the work involved does not make their culture worthwhile. In our growing conditions these iris need to be potted and the pot kept in a warm dry spot during summer. After active autumn growth they again require storage in cool dry conditions during winter. They need a sunny growing position with sharp drainage so ground or pot preparation is important. Over a base of gravel or crushed rock a mixture of garden soil and coarse sand well sweetened with dolomite and well fertilised provides the best medium.

Growing oncocyclus iris is, to understate the case, difficult, but experimentation and persistence can be rewarded with spectacular results. The typical oncocyclus flower is borne singly and often looks disproportionate as the strongly recurved falls appear small by comparison with the upright standards. The patterns and markings are unique in the iris world and most flowers carry large signal patches.

Iris susiana (the Mourning Iris) is the best known and most often grown oncocyclus species. It has a cream ground, veined, dotted and stippled brown-purple with large dark purple signals and brown-black beards.

Iris gatesii has a green-grey base with pale inconspicuous violet veins and mustard beards.

Iris paradoxa has violet base colour, veined darker and dark purple beards.

Regelia Iris

Regelia iris are natives of Russia and Afghanistan and although their cultivation requirements are similar to the oncocyclus they are somewhat less demanding. They have from one to three flowers on a spike.

Iris korolkowii (the Pagoda Iris) is the most common regelia. Base colour is a grey-cream with veining in varying shades of brown and both beards and signal patch of the same colour. There are several forms of *I. korolkowii*, some of which are species and some probably hybrids.

Iris hoogiana varies in colour from light blue to blue-violet with iridescent petals and gold beards.

Iris stolonifera also varies in colour, from lilac to blue to red-purple with veining in shades of brown. Beards are from blue to yellow.

There are many other pure arils but most are little known and little grown in this country.

Arilbred iris are again divided into two separate classes, those with 50% or more aril and those with less than 50% aril, commonly called Mohr-type arils.

Much of the work in hybridising arilbreds in Australia has been done by Sam Fankhauser in Victoria and Gordon Loveridge in New South Wales. Unfortunately the arilbreds, although easier to grow than the pure arils, have proven difficult and lack popularity because of this. Many of the hybrids are magnificent flowers of great beauty and in a colour patterning far different to the more popular bearded iris. Cultivars commercially available include:

'Jade', basically green with a blue and brown influence and flecking. Very distinctive but only part aril. This iris is very easy to grow and will do well wherever tall bearded iris are grown. **Plate 85.**
'Wind Shadows', in cream and brown, is another relatively easily grown cultivar.

Other named arilbreds are shown in Plates 86–89.

3 Louisiana Iris

The Louisiana iris are natives of the United States, being found in the swamps of Louisiana as four distinct species: *Iris fulva*, a tall plant with red toned flowers rather drooping in appearance; *Iris giganticaerulea*, an even taller plant with large blue flowers that flare; *Iris brevicaulis (foliosa)*, a low growing plant with blue and white flowers, well substanced on branched stems, and *Iris nelsonii*, a large tall plant with flowers similar in colour to *I.fulva*. It has branched stems, and colours range from yellow through to red with double-budded sockets.

From these four species hybridisers have given us the magnificent garden plants readily available today. All of the original hybridising was done in the United States, but in recent years Bob Raabe, Myrtle Murray, Craig Carroll, Janet Hutchinson and, in particular, John Taylor—all from New South Wales—have produced superb quality Louisiana iris. The improvement in these iris has been startling and much of the credit for this improvement goes to John Taylor, who has done much to develop the form and substance of the flower and to improve the bud count of the spike, resulting in a longer flowering period.

Cultivation

Louisiana iris will grow well throughout Australia and New Zealand, but are at their best in warm, humid climates where the bearded iris do not fare so well. Spectacular results can be obtained with these beauties in the northern coastal areas of New South Wales and throughout Queensland coastal areas. Some Louisiana iris are frost tender but most, if not all, will tolerate light frost and all will grow in cool climates if well mulched in autumn. They are rather adaptable to situation, requiring sun to give the best performance but growing well in filtered sunlight, particularly in hot climates. Probably the most important requirements of Louisiana iris are an acid soil and adequate water in the growing season.

Ground preparation is essential to achieve satisfactory results. Louisiana iris like a rich, heavy soil, so large quantities of compost or well rotted animal manure can be incorporated in the soil if it is deficient. Many growers prepare an acid bed, which consists of an area dug out to spade depth lined with plastic sheets with sulphur incorporated into the replaced soil.

Louisiana iris grow actively in spring and autumn. I have found a certain degree of summer dormancy but no doubt plants can be kept growing well in summer if adequate water is provided. During the growing period they require a lot of water and for this reason can be grown in standing water or in pots placed in ponds (Plate 90). They are gross feeders and can be heavily composted and fed with well rotted animal manures (be careful of fowl manure as it could be too alkaline), chemical fertilisers suitable for azaleas and camellias or cotton-seed meal. These iris need to be mulched in summer as protection against heat and in winter as protection against frost. Suitable mediums are bark, leaves and acid compost, all of which give protection to the rhizomes which are inclined to rise toward the surface. For this reason they are best planted 3–5cm below the surface and other planting instructions are similar to those for tall bearded iris. The incorporation of an 8–9 month slow release fertiliser at planting time is recommended.

In suitable growing conditions many of the Louisiana iris are rampant growers, needing dividing and replanting after 2–3 years in the ground. This process is much the same as described for tall bearded iris and is best achieved in March or April, although there is an argument for dividing Louisiana iris in November immediately after they have flowered. Good strong plants can be moved throughout most of the year without any harm.

Because of their rampant growth Louisiana iris can be invasive so care should be taken to plant them sufficiently far apart to keep them apart. For vigorous varieties 60cm should be allowed.

Pests and Diseases

Pests causing problems with Louisiana iris are much the same as those dealt with in the section on tall bearded iris and should be treated the same way.

Louisiana iris are not subject to many disease problems, although they can be devastated by those two common problems, rust and leaf spot. Both of these were discussed in the tall bearded iris section but it is perhaps worthwhile to make further mention here. Treatment is with any suitable fungicide—Mancozeb seems to be the most effective—and it should be applied quickly and at weekly intervals if either of the problems arise. Prevention would be regarded as far more acceptable than cure, which is often very difficult, and here there are many theories as to the best methods of preventing these most serious diseases.

My own theory is that weather conditions and not soil conditions have the most effect on leaf spot, and since the weather is beyond our control the best approach is clean cultivation, provision of the best possible growing conditions, a regular preventative spraying program and vigilance. If leaf spot does occur, and it will on certain cultivars in humid weather or when cool nights are followed by warm days, then removal of the infected leaves and treatment of the others is advisable.

It is well known that certain cultivars are more susceptible to leaf spot than others and I would strongly recommend that only those with a certain inbuilt resistance should be grown. It is indeed unfortunate that the time of greatest vulnerability to leaf spot seems to correspond with bloom and the time immediately preceding bloom. It gives little joy to see the clump at bloom time decimated by unhealthy foliage. For this reason I would rate quite a few popular Louisiana iris very low as garden subjects and I see no future for any Louisiana iris unless it has this inbuilt resistance to disease.

If, as I suggest, the cause of leaf spot is climatic and the very climates in which these iris do so well are the types of climate to promote disease, then hybridisers will have to place health very high on their priority list before plants are introduced.

The Louisiana iris is an ideal garden plant for a bog situation or for growing in standing water. For this reason many gardeners like to grow them in pots. Potted plants are beautiful in flower and give accent to a pool at any time of the year but care must be taken with the mixture used. Pots should be as large as possible to cope with the vigorous growth and the mixture should be of garden soil, peat moss, compost and well rotted manure in about equal proportions. It should be fertile and an 8–9 month slow release fertiliser should be incorporated in the soil at planting time.

Landscaping with Louisiana Iris

Plants that make suitable companions for Louisiana iris in standing water include water lilies, both the hardy and tropical types; water hyacinth, water poppy, water lettuce, duckweed, lobelia cardinalis, papyrus, arum lilies, Green Goddess lily and water hibiscus. As marginal or bog plants, arum lily, Green Goddess lily and papyrus are suitable.

Whites

'Helen Naish' is an outstanding round-formed sparkling white with green veins and green influence in the petals. Ruffled flowers in abundance. Healthy and vigorous. This iris was bred in Australia by John Taylor and in 1985 was the recipient of the first Australasian Dykes Medal—the highest award given to any iris. **Plate 91.**

'Clara Goula' is the parent of 'Helen Naish'. This is a well formed, tall, vigorous and healthy grower that produces show spikes displaying ruffled flowers in creamy white. **Plate 92.**

'Dural White Butterfly' is purest of pure white.

'White Umbrella' is a huge white with gold veins.

'First Favourite' is a very heavily ruffled and rounded white.

Creams

'Monument' is an attractive rounded light cream-yellow. Healthy.

'Danza' is a creamy white with green-yellow veins.

'Ice Magic' is a cream with darker veins and orangeline signals.

'Bellevue Butterfly' is a tall, ruffled cream.

'Gaia' is a warm creamy yellow.

'Selena' is cream with green-yellow veins.

'Soft Laughter' is a warm cream with gold signals and green veins.

Yellows

'Dural Charm' is close to the ultimate in Louisiana iris. This bright canary yellow flower is beautifully formed, rounded and lightly ruffled. The blooms are produced in abundance on a medium plant, healthy and vigorous. This iris was bred in Australia by John Taylor and is a Dykes Medal winner. **Plate 93.**

'Lucille Holley' is a very tall well branched iris with excellent growth and spikes. Colour is a soft creamy-yellow with a buff influence, and the form is superb.

'Alluvial Gold' is a mid-yellow with deeper midribs.

'Classical Note' is a light gold-yellow with deeper veins.

'Fat Tuesday' is a broad, rounded butter-gold.

'Green Elf' is a clear yellow with a green influence.

'Koorawatha' is a superb, multibudded, mid-yellow with ruffles and show spikes.

'Noble Planet' is a heavily-ruffled creamy-yellow with darker veins and styles.

Orange-Tans

'Fine Warrior' is a greyed orange-tan with a yellow star-shaped centre.

'Gladiator's Gift' is a mid chocolate-brown, heavily ruffled and rounded.

'Valera' is a soft brown that does not fade. Flower form, health, vigour and bud placement are all excellent. This is an outstanding new iris. **Plate 94.**

Reds

'Ann Chowning' is a very dark red with a prominent yellow signal. The flower is large, slightly recurved and well formed. The plant is vigorous and healthy. A great iris. **Plate 95.**

'Frank Chowning' is a soft red on shorter spikes.

'Parade Music' is a dark red with shorter spikes.

'Piece de Resistance' is an orange red.

'Professor Jim' is a rose-red tetraploid.

'Top Notch' is a mid-red.

'Warramunda' is a pale red with yellow veins.

'Wine and Dine' is a deep wine-red.

'Wine Country' is a burgundy.

Pinks

'Screen Gem' is a large, imposing, well formed mid-pink flower.

'All Agaze' is a light pink and salmon bitone.

'Dawn Planet' is a fancy pink bitone.

'Dancing Vogue' is a sensational clear mid-pink of outstanding form. **Plate 96.**

'Margaret Hunter' is another top pink with a slight mauve influence. Tall, healthy and vigorous plants produce flowers in abundance. **Plate 97.**

'Natural Wonder' is a dusky pink. Flowers are large with wavy ruffles. **Plate 98.**

'Patient Reward' is a mid-pink of great vigour.

'Watch Out' is a magenta bitone with outstanding growth and vigour. Top award winner. **Plate 99.**

'**Josephine Shanks**' is a beautiful, rounded mid-pink with a star centre.

'**Edith Fear**' is a superbly formed pink bitone with cream styles and a cream influence in the sepals. Growth is adequate, plant is healthy and vigorous. This is a very popular iris bred in Australia by John Taylor. **Plate 100.**

'**Commandment**' is a glowing bitone with pink sepals and rosy magenta-pink petals edged in pink. Superb flower form is rounded and ruffled on a plant that is healthy and vigorous. This is a top quality iris bred in Australia by John Taylor. **Plate 101.**

Blues

'**Quiet Harbour**' is a sky-blue.

'**Cammeray**' is a light blue.

'**Exquisite Lady**' is a mid-blue with a silver rim.

'**Brookvale Nocturne**' is a top quality mid-blue-violet iris with a white influence. Form, growth, health and vigour are all top class. This iris was bred in Australia by Myrtle Murray. **Plate 102.**

'**Eolian**' is a real sky-blue—beautiful colour on a plant that grows well and is always healthy.

'**Clyde Remond**' has small ruffled flowers of rich cornflower-blue—a colour which absolutely glows. Plant growth is correspondingly small, but it is vigorous and healthy.

'**Gulf Shores**' is a short, mid to dark blue.

'**Sinfonietta**' is a rich mid-blue.

'**Poseidon's Pool**' is a tall dark blue.

'**La Perouse**' is a medium sized rich cobalt blue. Growth is excellent, colour is superb and really glows, form is good but the substance is only average. This fault is readily forgiven when one sees the colour. This iris, bred by Bob Raabe, was the first Australian-raised iris to receive international acclaim. **Plate 103.**

'**Sea Consul**' is a sky-blue, with white centre and rim.

'**Sea Lord**' is a sensational rounded dark blue. **Plate 104.**

'**Malibu Magic**' is a blue bitone with feathering.

Purples

'**Glittering Prize**' is a dark purple bitone.

'**Honoured Guest**' is purple with a light edge and reverse.

'**Purple Pallas**' is a purple bitone with a serrated edge.

'**Barossa**' is a smoky purple with an unusual gloss and sheen.

'**C'est Chic**' is red-violet. **Plate 105.**

'**Concours Elegance**' is plum-purple to magenta.

'**Full Eclipse**' is very dark, near black.

'**Jazz Ballet**' is a sensational dark violet to purple, heavily ruffled and beautifully formed with a large star centre. Winner of all the top awards. **Plate 106.**

''**Bout Midnight**' is the darkest yet. Close to black. **Plate 107.**

'**Good Vibes**' is a large purple self with a yellow star cente.

'**John's Lucifer**' Very dark red-purple. **Plate 108.**

'**Louie**' is a dark blue-purple.

'**Lina**' is a heavily ruffled, greyed violet.

'**Satchmo**' is a dark black-purple. Tall.

'**Midnight Drama**' is a ruffled purple with a star centre and lighter reverse.

'**Mighty Rich**' is a low growing deep red purple of beautiful form. Growth is adequate, disease resistance has yet to be tested fully, but early indications are that the plant is healthy.

'**Professor Ike**' and '**Professor Claude**' are two new and outstanding irises. They are the first tetraploid Louisiana irises on the market and are very similar. Each is a dark red purple of huge proportions. Big foliage, big flowers and lovely form make these iris show stoppers. 'Ike' is a better grower than 'Claude'. Health and vigorous are unsurpassed. **Plate 109.**

'**Jeri**' is a dark grape-purple.

Others

'**Flight of Fantasy**' White sepals edged blue-violet, violet petals edged lighter. Yellow signals surrounded by white. Unique. **Plate 110.**

'**Mrs Ira Nelson**' has for many years set the standard for Louisiana iris. It is best described as a lavender orchid or mineral violet. Colour is lovely and the large, heavily substanced and beautifully formed flowers are born in abundance on tall healthy and vigorous spikes that often open three flowers simultaneously to make this the perfect show iris. It is worthy of every superlative one can envisage. **Plate 176.**

'**Bob Ward**' White and lavender-pink bicolour.

'**Jet Ace**' has white sepals and yellow petals.

'**Old South**' Cream-veined and washed overall with light violet.

'**Perfect Match**' is a rosy magenta bitone with green cente and yellow signals.

'**Rosebery**' has white-veined yellow-green sepals and pale yellow petals.

'**Desert Jewel**' A sensational, multicoloured beauty. **Plate 111.**

'**C'est-si-bon**' is in a class of its own. The very large flowers are violet with a strong white ray pattern and white edge to the petals giving a plicata effect. Growth is strong, plants vigorous and the superb spikes hold many blooms in double-budded sockets. This is one of John Taylor's great hybridising successes. **Plate 112.**

'**Top Start**' Blue and violet bicolour. It has medium sized flowers of great form with heavy ruffling. **Plate 113.**

'**Margaret Lee**' A round and ruffled beauty of variable colouration from pink-mauve to violet with sepals variable and often marbled. Great parent for different colours. **Plate 114.**

'**Art World**' is an unusual mauve-pink with excellent form. **Plate 115.**

'**Our Parris**' is a soft apricot-pink blend fading to pale creamy apricot. **Plate 116.**

'**Bayou Mystique**' Lavender and violet bicolour. Tall and multibudded.

4 Californian Iris

The Californian iris—previously called Pacific Coast iris—are natives of the western coast of the United States. These delightful small iris are mainly derived from four species: *Iris innominata, I. douglasiana, I. tenax* and *I. munzii*. They are, in general, evergreen and form small, compact plants which send up flowers over an extended period in early to mid-spring. Height of spike is variable and ranges from as low as 10cm to as tall as 90cm. **Plates 117, 118.**

Iris douglasiana

Iris douglasiana is the most adaptable of the Californian iris and is widely grown. It is a hardy plant, sun tolerant, vigorous and floriferous. *I. douglasiana* is not particular about soil conditions and forms a solid circular mass of foliage under normal growing conditions. Flowering spikes are tall and branched and carry up to three flowers in a colour range of creams, yellows, mauves, lavenders and purples, often with spray patterns and eye markings.

Iris innominata

Iris innominata is found naturally in rich, well drained acid soil. It is a hardy plant, sun tolerant and frost tolerant. *I. innominata* requires a fair amount of moisture in spring but likes to dry out in summer. Plant growth is neat and flowering spikes are up to 40cm tall, unbranched and carrying up to two flowers per stem. Flower colour range is yellow, mauve, lavender and purple, often veined and netted.

Iris tenax

Iris tenax is an easily grown, adaptable plant, hardy and sun tolerant. Leaf growth is tall, often taller than the flowering spikes which are up to 50cm tall. Spikes are unbranched and the blooms, carried singly, are in yellow, mauve, blue, lavender and purple.

Iris munzii

Iris munzii comes from partially shaded areas, with moist soil conditions. It is vigorous but tender in heavy frost areas. Flowering spikes are up to 70cm high, above the foliage which grows to 50cm. Flowers vary from lavender through blue to violet.

Other Californian iris species include *I. bracteata, I. chrysophylla, I. fernaldii, I. hartwegii, I. macrosiphon, I. purdyi* and *I. tenuissima*.

Cultivation

Most of the Californian iris available are hybrids developed from the intercrossing of the first four species. They like a woodland setting but will grow well in full sun. Soil should be well drained, neutral to slightly acid and well made up with humus. They require an adequate supply of moisture in winter and spring but are best suited to areas with a long dry summer. Drainage is important in cultivation but pests and diseases are normally not a problem.

Perhaps the most difficult problem in handling Californian iris is their resentment towards being moved. This makes division and propagation of named varieties a frustrating and often disastrous venture. These iris are best moved when the new white roots are forming—often, after a drying out period, the new root growth follows watering. This usually occurs in late May or early June in our milder climates but can vary greatly from any one season to the next, even in the same area.

Although little success has been achieved in vegetative increasing of Californian iris, they can be readily raised from seed. The species will come true to parent from seed but flowers of great diversity, fascinating in both form and colour, can be obtained by intercrossing the hybrids.

Dan Hargraves of Australia has been a world leader in developing the Californian iris and his work has, in recent years, been carried on by Chas Blyth and now his son Barry of Tempo Two Nursery in Victoria and by my wife Helen in New South Wales. There is now available in Australia the finest collection of Californian iris in the world. The above hybridisers have not been quick to name, propagate and introduce their iris and their first named cultivars were released only in 1983.

Production of hybrids from seed is easy as the plants readily set seed, both naturally and when crossed by hand. Seed should be collected when the pod hardens and browns, before it splits, and seed planted in autumn will germinate during winter and spring. Seeds can be planted in seed raising mix in pots or directly in the ground where they will flower in the season of the year following planting. If planted in pots the seedlings will have to be planted out and this can mean large losses unless great care is taken. Plants set out in April or May the year following crossing will often bloom in September and form good size clumps in the following season.

As there are only a few named varieties available at this stage there can be no long list of recommendations, but no potential grower will go astray by using plants or sowing seed obtained from plants that are derivatives of the Hargraves breeding program.

Seed pod splitting to show seed

Named plants are available from Joe Ghio in California, who has incorporated the Hargraves line into his breeding program, but my only venture in importing Californian iris was a dismal failure so I have settled for seed raising ventures in recent years. **Plates 119–129.**

5 Spuria Iris

Spuria iris are found naturally in southern Europe, north Africa and into Asia Minor. Those available to gardeners are the species *I. spuria, I. ochroleuca, I. monnieri, I. crocea, I. maritima* and hybrids from these. More demanding in their cultural requirements and less frequently grown are the dwarf species *I. graminea, I. sintenisii* and *I. kernerana.*

The flowers of the spuria iris resemble those of the bulbous iris (Dutch iris) but they are held on taller spikes and usually display two or more flowers open simultaneously down the spikes. Their height, compactness of clump, graceful presentation of flowers and bloom production make them ideal specimens for the rear of the perennial border or for growing as individual clumps with shrubs as a backdrop and annuals in the foreground. Indeed the spuria irises form an invaluable garden perennial group as they are beautiful in flower, and neat and tidy with attractive sword-like foliage at other times in the growing season. The foliage dies down quickly after flowering only to send up new, clean shoots almost immediately. **Plates 130, 131.**

Flowering time in our climate is October through into November followed by summer dormancy. They have attractive clean foliage in the winter months when good bright colour is scarce.

Iris ochroleuca and *Iris monnieri*

Iris ochroleuca grows to 1.4m with large white flowers and a large yellow signal. Spikes are branched and carry several flowers. This iris is very hardy and prolific. *Iris monnieri* is basically a rich yellow in colour and although given species status it is quite likely that it is a natural hybrid.

Cultivation

Most of the species are neither easy nor predictable but there are many hybrids available that are excellent garden subjects. Spuria iris require full sun, good drainage and ample water in the growing season. Water must be withdrawn in the summer dormant period or the new shoots being formed are inclined to rot. Consequently, in the Sydney area, high humidity and frequent rain in January and February often combine to cause havoc among the spurias but otherwise they are easy plants to grow.

The spuria iris grow best in slightly alkaline soil so the addition of dolomite to acid or neutral soils is desirable. Although not particular as to soil conditions spuria iris are heavy feeders and will respond to the addition of compost, manure and chemical fertilisers.

Spuria iris resent being moved and will often take two years to flower after being planted initially or divided. For this reason they should be planted in a permanent position, with allowance made for expansion of the clump, and then left alone for several years. Care should be taken with new plants or those being divided to ensure that the roots do not dry out at any stage as this is normally fatal.

Hybridising the spurias is not difficult as they set seed readily and a reasonable percentage of germination is obtained in the first year. From then on events slow down and even if plants are set out in ideal conditions bloom is not usually experienced until the third or fourth season. If seedlings are germinated in pots they should not be planted out until well established and then only moved in autumn.

If good parents are used the resulting seedlings are often of good quality and selection of seedlings to be retained is often difficult. In looking at individual flowers observe the following points—standards should be erect and falls flared; faults are elongated claws or gaposis (a gap between the style arm and the haft of the falls). Spikes should have classic flower placement with no elongated branching, be erect and strong. **See Plates 132, 133, 134.**

Pests and Diseases

Mustard seed fungus is a frequent problem with spurias in warm, wet weather. It can wipe out a complete clump and is difficult, in fact well nigh impossible to control if conditions are favourable for its spread. A recommended method of treatment is to lift the rhizomes, scrape clean and dry and then treat with Condy's crystals (potassium permanganate).

Prevention is better than cure and while we have no control over weather conditions the best management of spurias involves growing them in raised beds, mixing coarse sand into the soil and incorporating Terrachlor into the soil before planting. The use of an 8–9 month slow release fertiliser should also maintain a regular nitrogen supply to the plant without the over-indulgence which could make the spurias prone to rot or fungus infection.

'Amber Ripples' Pale blue and amber.
'Barbara's Kiss' Burgundy-mauve.
'Dawn Candle' A well formed yellow and white iris with all good garden qualities.
'Archie Owen' Rich yellow with wide petals giving a new dimension to spuria iris.

'Missouri Gal' Blue.

'New Harmony' Brown and yellow.

'Northern Muse' Dark blue-violet.

'Objet d'Art' White.

'Satin Wood' Dark brown.

'Blue Bunting' Purple standards and yellow falls rimmed purple.

'Blue Lassie' Blue with a white infusion.

'Bronzing' Violet with a bronze overlay.

'Ila Crawford' A near white self with a minimum of yellow. Beautifully formed flower with the bonus of ruffled petals. **Plate 135.**

'Butter Chocolate' Brown, with a gold blaze.

'Chestnut Chime' Chocolate-brown.

'Dress Circle' Blue-violet standards and yellow falls rimmed white.

'Elan Vital' Cream.

'Forty Carats' Gold.

'Full Sun' Yellow.

'Happy Choice' Pale blue with gold on falls.

'Heart to Heart' Blue.

'Highline Amethyst' Reddish purple.
'Minneopa' has blue standards and yellow falls.

'Highline Halo' Yellow with a white border.

'Highline Lavender' Light lavender-purple.

'Just Reward' Mid-blue.

'Sahara Sands' is a light brown of lovely form. There is virtually no signal. **Plate 136.**

'Fort Ridge' is a top quality dark blue with ruffled petals. **Plate 137.**

'Social Circle' White with a yellow signal.

'Son of Sun' Yellow.

'Struttin'' Yellow shaded amber.

'Tiger Blues' Blue-lavender with brown veins.

6 Siberian Iris

The Siberian iris are derived mainly from two species, *I. sibirica* and *I. sanguinea*, both of which are found growing naturally in Siberia although the former is more common in central Europe. These form the basis for the 28-chromosome group of Siberian iris, which constitute most of those commonly grown. There is also a 40-chromosome group of species and hybrids derived mainly from *I. chrysophages, I. bulleyana, I. delavayi, I. wilsonii, I. forrestii, I. clarkei, I. dykesii* and *I. phragmitetorum*.

As the former are more easily grown, their hybrids more readily available, and because they are a more rewarding garden proposition, discussion will be restricted to their cultural requirements.

Cultivation

The Siberian iris are deciduous perennials which grow best in climates with a cold, somewhat dry winter but they require ample water in the growing season. At no stage should the plants be allowed to dry out, a very important point when planting or dividing clumps. They are best moved or planted in autumn or early spring and should be planted in well prepared, composted rich soil which should preferably be neutral or slightly acid, although these iris will grow and flower well in slightly alkaline soil.

Siberian iris prefer a situation in full sun but they will tolerate partial shade. They are not bog or water plants and should be planted in a situation where they will remain for some years as they form a mat of roots and are not easy to move once established.

Good rich soil and a covering of compost ensure good growth of Siberian iris. They respond to organic gardening and chemical fertiliser should be kept to a minimum. If well mulched the soil will retain moisture and promote good growth.

Plants die right down over winter so their position in the garden should be marked. With the return of warm weather in the spring the new growth commences and is immediately attractive. The bright green, thin reedy foliage is attractive in the garden throughout the growing season and is further enhanced in late spring when the graceful flowers come into bloom.

Siberian iris come in white, shades of blue, violet and purple. There has been development in the burgundy-red tones and recently yellow amoenas and the start of yellow lines have appeared. Older hybrids have flowers with arched to drooping petals but modern varieties tend to a more flared form with a corresponding improvement in substance. Many cultivars are well branched, producing up to 6 or more flowers to a spike and a continuation of bloom in the garden. A clump of Siberian iris in full bloom is a magnificent sight equalled by very few garden perennials, particularly when they sway to and fro in a gentle breeze.

A new race of induced tetraploid cultivars is now becoming available. These new plants are still very expensive but should become more readily available and correspondingly less expensive in the next few years.

Hybridising and growing on the resultant seedlings is relatively easy. The flowers cross readily so care must be taken to ensure a planned cross is actually effected. Pods naturally pollinated (bee pods) are easily set, so for certain accuracy, flowers should be bagged or covered before opening, petals removed on making the cross and then the pollinated flower recovered.

Seed sets readily from planned crosses and the pod forms quickly. Pods ripen in January–February and should be harvested when they start to brown in colour. Seed is best stored and then planted in April—it should not be left any later as viability is lost. Germination is quick and efficient; there is often a quantity of seedlings growing well before winter, but in order to avoid losses young plants should not be set out the first season. The seedlings should be kept growing and well watered for the next year whereupon they can be planted out in the following autumn. A fair percentage will then flower in spring. The bloom season is short and spectacular—a mass of bloom over a 2 to 3 week period—although hybridisers are working on producing reblooming varieties. Initial indications are that these rebloomers will, after a brief rest period, rebloom in early to mid-summer. Growing Siberian iris from seed is easy and rewarding in terms of quantity but many of the resulting seedlings are look-alikes with progress in the development of new forms and colours and in the improvement of those in existence relatively slow. The Siberian iris are virtually untroubled by pests and diseases and are excellent garden plants if your climatic conditions are suitable for their culture.

'Anniversary' Classic white Siberian of good form and substance. Grows well, flowers well, sets seed readily and is a good parent. **Plate 138.**

'White Swirl' Another quality white with all good garden attributes.

'Vi Luihn' Tall growing, lustrous rich blue-purple of excellent form and good growth. Lovely.

'Alter Ego' Pale blue with dark blue markings.

'Butter and Sugar' Creamy white and yellow.

'Cleve Dodge' Light blue bitone.

'Ausable River' Rich flaring blue-violet. Very vigorous and reliable.

'Coolabah' Wine-rose with white on falls.

'Fourfold White' White.

'Marilyn Holmes' Ruffled and flared rich violet-blue. Very vigorous and an excellent bloomer.

'Navy Brass' Tetraploid. Rich dark navy-blue blazed gold. Spectacular.

'Frosty Rim' Dark blue with a silver edge.

'Halcyon Seas' Dark blue bitone.

'I'm Just Blue' Royal blue.

'Maggie Smith' Pinkish violet.

'Music Royal' Large royal blue.

'Pink Haze' Mauve-pink.

'Pink Sparkle' White and pink.

'Swank' Mid-blue of good quality, compact form and good garden habits.

'Pirate Prince' Purple.

'Rose Quest' Orchid-rose.

'Showdown' Red-grape.

'Temper Tantrum' Dark red-purple.

'White Magnificence' A tall white.

'Wing on Wing' White.

'Ego' is a ruffled flaring deep mid-blue. **Plate 139.**

'Super-Ego' has pale blue standards and dark blue falls which shade to white at the edges. **Plate 140.**

'Orville Fay' is a large mid-blue tetraploid iris of good form and growth. **Plate 141.**

7 Bulbous Iris

The bulbous iris form a group quite distinct from the other iris already discussed which are grown from rhizomes. Whereas a rhizome will flower only once and produce increase, the true bulbs will flower year after year and increase by forming tiny bulblets which bloom in two years.

Iris xiphium

The most commonly grown bulbous iris are the xiphiums, made up of the species *I. xiphium, I. lusitanica, I. tingitana, I. filifolia, I. fontanesii, I. juncea, I. boissieri, I. taitii* and *I. latifolium*. The iris known and grown commercially as Dutch iris are hybrids of *I. xiphium, I. fontanesii, I. filifolia* and *I. tingitana*, while those known as Spanish iris are derivatives of *I. xiphium*. Of all the bulbous iris the Dutch iris are, by far, the easiest to grow and even though they excel in cooler climates they will grow well in warmer, more humid areas like Sydney. Ironically, they are not natives of Holland—together with the Spanish iris they come from the western Mediterranean area. Much of the early hybridising at the beginning of the twentieth century was done by the Dutch bulb growers, hence the name.

Cultivation

Dutch iris grow best in a sunny position in well drained slightly alkaline soil. They should be planted to a depth of three times their own length, usually in the months March, April or May. Later planting will slow down initial growth and ensure winter protection, particularly in cold areas. These iris do not require a great deal of fertiliser and get by with a dressing of blood and bone or bulb fertiliser and the addition of dolomite to acid soils.

Bulbs will flower progressively from late winter right through September and often into October in mild climates and can be left in the ground for the following season as long as they experience a dry and somewhat hot summer. If they are grown in a climate where there is plentiful summer rain they are best lifted after they die down and stored. Care must be taken with stored bulbs; they should be placed in a dry, well ventilated position, covered with dry sand or vermiculite, and periodically dusted with a fungicide and sprayed with Metasystox. This will control shrivelling, mould and aphids. Bulbs should not be left out of the ground for a long time.

Pests and Diseases

Probably the greatest single problem in growing the xiphiums is their susceptibility to a virus which infects the bulbs and weakens them, causing distortion of the foliage, streaking in the flowers and eventual death of the bulb. There is no cure and infected bulbs should be burned. Prevention is the only answer and as the virus is transmitted by aphids they must be controlled. Metasystox, because of its residual systemic action, is the best spray to use.

Mustard seed fungus can be a problem with bulbous iris just as it can be with most rhizomatous iris if the conditions are to its liking—warm humid weather. Its treatment has been discussed previously (page 42).

The xiphiums can be grown easily from seed, which will not, however, be true to the parent. Seed germinates readily but bulbs grown from seed will take four years to bloom.

All are excellent cut flowers and there is a large market for their production. In the garden they are best grown in clumps of ten or more.

All Dutch iris are susceptible to virus but the following varieties are the most resistant and hence the best garden propositions.

'Golden Harvest' This is by far the healthiest and best formed of the Dutch iris although the flowers are somewhat smaller than the other commercial varieties. Flowering mid-season this rich golden-yellow is thoroughly reliable and quite vigorous. **Plate 142.**

'**Wedgwood Blue**' is an early flowering mid-blue of good form, size and vigour. It is a relatively healthy variety.

'**Imperator**' flowers late and is a clean healthy blue of good form and vigour.

'**Professor Blaauw**' is a rich dark blue that flowers mid-season to late. Flowers are large and very impressive but disease resistance is only average. **Plate 143.**

'**White Perfection**' is the best in this colour. It is not as vigorous as the others mentioned but is relatively disease-free.

'**Bronze Queen**' is an unusual bronze colour. The medium sized flowers are well formed and the bulbs are reasonably vigorous and disease free.

There are others not regularly available on a commercial basis, although 'Lilac Queen', 'Purple Sensation' and 'Marquet' have been on sale recently. **Plates 144, 145.**

Iris latifolium

A further irony occurs with the naming of the derivatives of *I. latifolium* as English iris, because these iris are natives of France and Spain. They come from cool mountain country and require a moist, slightly acid soil. These iris make large bulbs which should be planted to a depth three times their length and then left in the ground as the bulbs are easily damaged and deteriorate quickly if left out of the ground. If you are lifting bulbs for dividing or planting for the first time do so as soon as possible after flowering. Bulbs should be well watered in the growing season and kept damp in summer.

Their general care is otherwise similar to the Dutch iris. English iris are larger flowered than the Dutch, flower much later in the season, usually in late November through into December, and are not suitable for warm, humid coastal areas where they will not flower. They are particularly suitable for the cold winter inland areas of the southern mainland states, Tasmania and the south island of New Zealand, and make excellent cut flowers. I have not seen or heard of named varieties being available but seedlings in white, shades of blue, purple, pink and lavender are occasionally listed for sale.

Iris reticulata

The reticulatas, consisting of the species *I. reticulata*, *I. histrio*, *I. histrioides*, *I. danfordiae*, *I. vartanii* and *I. bakerana*, are dwarf bulbous iris that are natives of the Middle East and Asia Minor. They require a cold climate and hot dry summer and are best grown in a rich, composted, well drained and slightly alkaline soil in full sun.

Bulbs are best planted in autumn to a depth three times their size and they should be well watered in winter and spring. They will flower in late winter and early spring and should be allowed to dry out in summer. Their care and maintenance is, in all other aspects, similar to other bulbs and they are easily grown in the right climatic conditions. I have seen beautiful displays of these low-growing bulbs in the Leura and Mt Wilson area of New South Wales' Blue Mountains region but they fail in warm coastal areas. These iris can be grown easily from seed which takes a minimum of four years to bloom or from increase from bulblets which is quicker. *I. danfordiae* is sterile and will not propagate from seed. **Plate 146.**

Junos

The junos consist of about sixty species, some of which are *I. rosenbachiana*, *I. aucheri*, *I. postii*, *I. magnifica*, *I. stocksii*, *I. caucasica*, *I. graeberana*, *I. orchioides*, *I. warleyensis*, *I. fosterana*, *I. nicolai*, *I. palaestina*, *I. persica* and *I. planifolia*. They are natives of Central Asia and the Mediterranean (*I. planifolia*) and require a cold winter and hot dry summer and autumn. They require moderate watering in winter and spring and have the same cultural requirements as the reticulatas.

Bulbs multiply quickly and can be divided after four years. Care should be taken when lifting the fragile bulbs as damaged bulbs are often lost.

8 Evansia Iris

Evansia iris are distinguished from other iris in having a crest of petaloid tissue running linearly on each of the falls. This crest can be described as fimbriated, serrated or toothed in different varieties and may be orange, yellow or white. Members of this group are often called crested iris. The evansia iris are natives of Asia (China and Japan) and North America and form one of the most delicate, dainty and beautiful groups of the iris family.

Iris japonica

Cultivation

This delightful woodland plant revels in a rich slightly acid soil in a sheltered semi-shaded position. It needs protection from frost and hot afternoon sun so is best naturalised under trees. *Iris japonica* is ideal for temperate climates but can be grown in cold climates in greenhouses or under protection. This iris is a gross feeder (it should be kept well mulched at all times) and can be fertilised with well rotted cow manure or any complete azalea and camellia food.

Because of their similar cultural requirements *Iris japonica*, camellias and azaleas grown together present a glorious landscaping picture. *Iris japonica* flowers late in winter through to early spring and so comes into bloom with the spring-flowering double azaleas and the late *Camellia japonica* and early reticulatas. I can envisage the landscaping spectacle of a row of the reticulata camellia hybrid 'Valley Knudsen' underplanted with the azalea 'Comptesse de Kerchove' and then edged with *Iris japonica*.

This iris is evergreen and should be given adequate drainage and water throughout the year to keep the foliage healthy. Poor drainage can lead to fungus disease whereby the fan rots away from the rhizome which shrivels and dies.

In good conditions *Iris japonica* multiplies quickly and can become invasive. It flowers in August through September and into October in the Sydney area and can be divided or planted at any time of the year. The flowers are up to 8cm in diameter, rounded and ruffled with a fringed edge. They are a pale blue-lavender colour with orange markings on a white ground edged and dotted with a darker lavender-blue. Spikes grow to 60cm, are multibranched and carry between 20 and 30 flowers to a spike. Often 5 or 6 flowers will open simultaneously on a well grown spike. **Plates 147, 148.**

Apart from *I. japonica* itself there are the forms 'Uwodu', 'Ledger's Variety', a variegated leaf variety which is difficult to flower and evidently needs more sun than the plain leaf form, and the hybrids 'Nada' (a small white-flowered hybrid with *I. confusa*) and 'Darjeeling' (a larger lavender flower from 'Nada' self-crossed).

Iris confusa and Iris watii

These are similar species requiring the same general conditions as *I. japonica*. Their growth and flowers are somewhat larger (flowers up to 10cm in diameter); *I. watii* is a darker lavender-blue while *I. confusa* is paler—almost white. **Plate 149.** Two further similar hybrids are 'Queen's Grace', bred in New Zealand, and 'Bourne Graceful' from England. They are both worthwhile garden plants requiring similar conditions. **Plate 150.**

Iris milesii

Iris milesii is a hardy evansia whose foliage dies down in winter, so the plant will tolerate more frost. Flowers are light violet with darker markings and orange crests. They are somewhat smaller than those of *I. japonica* and flower over an extended period from late winter through to the end of spring. Cultural requirements are similar to those of *I. japonica*.

Iris tectorum

Iris tectorum (known as the roof iris) is a beautiful large flat and ruffled flower with white crests. It is vigorous, hardy and adaptable but requires protection from frost to perform at its best. Conditions similar to *I. japonica* are required; this iris is also a gross feeder which will quickly exhaust the soil unless it is heavily fertilised and kept well mulched. It requires plentiful water in the growing season and can easily be grown from seed which sets readily. **Plate 151.**

There is a white form with yellow crests which is a particularly beautiful iris but it is less vigorous and reluctant to bloom unless conditions are exactly to its liking.

The roof iris is so called because it is grown on the ridges of the roofs of thatched houses in some parts of Japan. There are two explanations for this, the first being that during a long-ago time of famine no soil was allowed to be used for anything else but growing food. The Japanese women made a face powder from the roots of the plant and, rather than do without their face powder, were forced to find an alternative place to cultivate it. The other explanation is that the iris roots were found to be an excellent medium to bind together the thatch and the wet clay used to complete the thatching process.

Iris gracilipes

Iris gracilipes is yet another woodland plant for cool to cold climates. It requires similar culture to the others in this section but is less tolerant of climatic conditions and does not do well in humid climates as experienced in Sydney. Small lilac flowers are produced in abundance in November if growing conditions are satisfactory. There is a white form but it is less vigorous and floriferous.

The American crested species *I. cristata, I. lacustris* and *I. tenuis* all require similar conditions to *I. gracilipes*. They are all hardier than the Asian species and relatively easy to grow in cooler areas of the country. Unfortunately they are not satisfactory garden plants in Sydney and milder more humid areas where *I. japonica, I. watii* and *I. tectorum* grow so well.

I. lacustris is a small plant with dainty slate-blue flowers, *I. cristata* is larger, brighter and the least demanding, while *I. tenuis* is taller and branched. I do not know of their availability but they are excellent garden specimens for the right conditions.

Iris blooms at Rainbow Ridge Nursery (p.7)

2. Iris blooms at Rainbow Ridge Nursery

3. Iris beds at Rainbow Ridge Nursery

. Tall bearded iris 'Mary Frances', Helen Grosvenor and Trixie the dachshund in the courtyard at Rainbow Ridge

5. Iris blooms at Rainbow Ridge Nursery

6. Mass planting of tall bearded iris at Rainbow Ridge Nursery

. Graeme Grosvenor with a championship-winning spike of the tall bearded iris 'Wedding Vow' (p.18)

. *(Right)* Alan Johnson at Rainbow Ridge with the iris that was later to bear his name (p.26)

9. 'White Lightning' (tall bearded) (p.18)

0. 'Leda's Lover' (tall bearded) (p.18)

1. *(Right)* 'Rellie' (tall bearded). Loveridge Medallion 1977; H.C., H.M., A.M. Bred by the author (p.18)

12. 'Crystalyn' (tall bearded) (p.18)

13. 'Toasted Almond' (tall bearded) (p.18)

14. 'Divine Duchess' (tall bearded) (p.19)

15. *(Right)* 'Full Tide' (tall bearded) (p.19)

16. 'Honkytonk Blues' (tall bearded) (p.19)

17. 'Silverado' (tall bearded) (p.19)

18. 'Dusky Challenger' (tall bearded) (p.20)

19. 'Lord Olivier' (tall bearded) (p.20)

20. 'Houdini' (tall bearded) (p.20)

21. 'Interpol' (tall bearded) (p.20)

23. 'Witches Sabbeth' (tall bearded) (p.20)

24. 'Mary Frances' (tall bearded) (p.20)

22. *(Left)* 'Bordello' (tall bearded) (p.20)

26. 'Orchidarium' (tall bearded) (p.20)

27. 'Rondetta' (tall bearded) (p.20)

25. *(Left)* 'Mary Frances' photographed in the author's courtyard

30. 'Lady Friend' (tall bearded) (p.21)

29. 'Persian Berry' (tall bearded) (p.21)

28. *(Left)* 'Taffeta Bow' (tall bearded) (p.21)

31. 'Flare Up' (tall bearded) (p.21)

32. 'Swain' (tall bearded) (p.21)

33. 'Rustler' (tall bearded) (p.22)

35. 'Metaphor' (tall bearded) (p.22)

36. 'Preface' (tall bearded) (p.22)

34. *(Left)* 'Mandolin' (tall bearded) (p.22)

37. 'Pink Taffeta' (tall bearded) (p.23)

38. 'Vanity' (tall bearded) (p.23)

39. 'Pink Belle' (tall bearded) (p.23)

40. 'Goddess' (tall bearded) (p.23)

41. *(Right)* 'Mollie Savell' (tall bearded) Bred by the author (p.23)

42. 'Prejudice' (tall bearded) (p.23)

43. 'New Moon' (tall bearded) (p.23)

44. 'Gold Country' (tall bearded) (p.24)

45. 'Joan McClemens' (tall bearded). Loveridge Medallion 1983; H.C., H.M., A.M. Bred by the author (p.24)

46. 'Temple Gold' (tall bearded) (p.24)

47. 'Radiant Energy' (tall bearded) (p.24)

48. 'Joyce Terry' (tall bearded) (p.24)

49. 'Song of Erin' (tall bearded) (p.24)

50. 'Rococo Valley' (tall bearded). Bred by Alan Johnson (p.25)

51. 'Going My Way' (tall bearded) (p.25)

53. 'Blue Staccato' (tall bearded) (p.26)

54. *(Right)* 'Circus Stripes' (tall bearded) (p.26)

52. *(Left)* 'Kiss' (tall bearded) (p.25)

55. 'Raspberry Fudge' (tall bearded) (p.26)

56. 'Jesse's Song' (tall bearded) (p.26)

57. *(Right)* 'Plum Gleam' (tall bearded) (p.26)

58. 'Smoke Rings' (tall bearded) (p.26)

59. 'Alan Johnson' (tall bearded). Loveridge Medallion 1979; H.C., H.M., A.M. Bred by the author (p.26)

60. 'Armada' (tall bearded). (p.26)

61. *(Left)* 'Secret Melody' (tall bearded) (p.26)

62. 'Snowbrook' (tall bearded) (p.26)

63. 'Asha Michelle' (tall bearded). Bred by Barry Blyth (p.26)

64. 'Rare Treat' (tall bearded) (p.26)

65. 'Blues Brothers' (tall bearded) (p.27)

66. 'Mystique' (tall bearded) (p.27)

67. 'Physique' (tall bearded) (p.27)

68. 'Floral Act' (tall bearded) (p.28)

69. 'All That Jazz' (tall bearded) (p.28)

70. 'Edith Wolford' (tall bearded) (p.28)

71. 'Latin Lark' (tall bearded) (p.28)

72. 'Planned Treasure' (tall bearded) (p.29)

73. 'San Jose' (tall bearded) (p.29)

74. 'Cameo Wine' (tall bearded). Bred by Barry Blyth. (p.29)

75. *(Right)* 'Michael Paul' (standard dwarf bearded) (p.30)

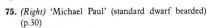

77. 'Wizard of Id' (standard dwarf bearded) (p.31)

76. *(Left)* 'Making Eyes' (standard dwarf bearded). Bred by Barry Blyth (p.30)

78. 'Zing Me' (intermediate bearded) (p.31)

81. 'Inner Circle' (border bearded) (p.32)

80. *(Left)* 'Pink Bubbles' (border bearded). (p.32)

79. 'Sundown Red' (intermediate bearded). Bred by Paul Blyth (p.31)

82. *(Left)* 'Elsedina' (border bearded). H.C., H.M., A.M. Bred by the author (p.32)

83. 'Curacao' (border bearded) (p.32)

84. 'Eye Magic' (border bearded) (p.32)

85. 'Jade' (part arilbred) (p.33)

86. 'Jewelled Veil' (arilbred) (p.33)

87. Unnamed sister seedling to 'Baghdad Note'. Bred by Barry Blyth. (p.33)

88. 'Ben Abou' (arilbred). Bred by Sam Fankhauser (p.33)

89. 'For Pleasure' (arilbred) (p.33)

90. *(Right)* Louisiana iris in a pond at Rainbow Ridge Nursery (p.34)

92. 'Clara Goula' (Louisiana) (p.35)

91. *(Left)* 'Helen Naish' (Louisiana) H.C., H.M. Bred by John Taylor (p.35)

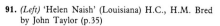

93. 'Dural Charm' (Louisiana). Loveridge Medallion 1982; H.C., H.M. Bred by John Taylor (p.36)

94. 'Valera' (Louisiana) (p.36)

95. 'Ann Chowning' (Louisiana) (p.36)

96. 'Dancing Vogue' (Louisiana) (p.36)

98. 'Natural Wonder' (Louisiana) (p.36)

99. 'Watch Out' (Louisiana) (p.36)

97. 'Margaret Hunter' (Louisiana) (p.36)

100. 'Edith Fear' (Louisiana). Loveridge Medallion 1981; H.C., H.M. Bred by John Taylor (p.37)

101. 'Commandment' (Louisiana). H.C., H.M. Bred by John Taylor (p.37)

102. 'Brookvale Nocturne' (Louisiana). H.C. Bred by Myrtle Murray (p.37)

103. 'La Perouse' (Louisiana). Bred by Bob Raabe (p.37)

104. 'Sea Lord' (Louisiana) (p.37)

105. 'C'est Chic' (Louisiana) (p.37)

106. 'Jazz Ballet' (Louisiana) (p.37)

107. ''Bout Midnight' (Louisiana) (p.37)

108. 'John's Lucifer' (Louisiana) (p.37)

109. 'Professor Ike' (Louisiana) (p.37)

110. 'Flight of Fantasy' (Louisiana) (p.38)

111. 'Desert Jewel' (Louisiana) (p.38)

112. 'C'est Si Bon' (Louisiana). H.C. Bred by John Taylor. (p.38)

113. 'Top Start' (Louisiana) (p.38)

114. 'Margaret Lee' (Louisiana) (p.38)

115. 'Art World' (Louisiana) (p.38)

116. 'Our Parris' (Louisiana) (p.38)

117. A clump of Californian iris (p.39)

118. A vase of mixed Californian iris (p.39)

119. Seedling Californian iris bred by Helen Grosvenor (p.40)

120. Seedling Californian iris bred by Helen Grosven (p.40)

121. Seedling Californian iris bred by Helen Grosvenor (p.40)

122. Seedling Californian iris bred by Helen Grosvenor (p.40)

123. Seedling Californian iris bred by Helen Grosvenor (p.40)

124. Seedling Californian iris bred by Helen Grosvenor (p.40)

125. Seedling Californian iris bred by Helen Grosvenor (p.40)

126. Seedling Californian iris bred by Barry Blyth. Photo Barry Blyth (p.40)

127. Seedling Californian iris bred by Barry Blyth (p.40)

128. A clump of Californian iris (p.40)

129. (Right) Californian iris plant in bloom (p.40)

130. A spike of spuria iris in the garden (p.41)

131. Spuria iris at Rainbow Ridge nursery (p.41)

132. Spike of spuria iris on the show bench. (p.42)

133. Spuria iris seedling bred by Helen Grosvenor (p.42)

134. Spuria iris seedling bred by Helen Grosvenor (p.42)

135. 'Ila Crawford' (spuria) (p.42)

136. 'Fort Ridge' (spuria) (p.42)

137. 'Sahara Sands' (spuria) (p.42)

138. 'Anniversary' (Siberian) (p.44)

139. 'Ego' (Siberian) (p.44)

140. 'Super Ego' (Siberian) (p.44)

141. 'Orville Fay' (Siberian) (p.44)

142. 'Golden Harvest' (Dutch) (p.46)

143. 'Professor Blaauw' (Dutch) (p.46)

144. 'Lilac Queen' (Dutch) (p.46)

145. 'Purple Sensation' (Dutch) (p.46)

146. Reticulata iris in a pot (p.46)

147. *Iris japonica* spike (p.41)

148. *Iris japonica* flower (p.47)

149. *Iris wattii* (p.47)

150. 'Bourne Graceful' (evansia) (p.47)

151. *Iris tectorum* (p.48)

152. Japanese iris at Rainbow Ridge Nursery (p.65)

153. Japanese iris at Rainbow Ridge Nursery (p.65)

154. 'Peacock Dance' (kaempferi) (p.68)

155. *(Right)* 'Time and Tide' (kaempferi) (p.68)

156. 'Akebono' (kaempferi) (p.68)

157. 'Chigogesho' (kaempferi) (p.68)

158. 'Dancing Waves' (kaempferi) (p.68)

159. 'Enchanting Melody' (kaempferi) (p.68)

160. 'Geisha Gown' (kaempferi) (p.68)

161. 'Ocean Mist' (kaempferi) (p.69)

162. 'Reign of Glory' (kaempferi) (p.69)

163. 'Rose Prelude' (kaempferi) (p.69)

164. 'Umi-Botaru' (kaempferi) (p.69)

165. 'Taga-Sode' (kaempferi) (p.70)

166. 'Syucho' (kaempferi) (p.70)

167. 'Hagoromo', white form (kaempferi) (p.70)

168. 'Hagoromo', white brushed lavender for (kaempferi) (p.70)

169. *Laevigata albopurpurea colchesterensis* (p.72)

170. *Laevigata albopurpurea monstrosa* (p.72)

171. *(Right) Iris virginica* (p.72)

172. *Iris foetidissima* (p.72)

173. *Iris unguicularis* 'Winsome' (p.72)

174. John Taylor holds a champion spike of the spuria iris 'Kyah Gold', bred by Barry Blyth (p.77)

175. Alan Johnson (left) from Australia and Keith Keppel (right) from the United States judging iris at the NSW Region of the Iris Society of Australia show (p.77)

176. A champion show spike of the Louisiana iris 'Mrs Ira Nelson' (pp.38 & 77)

177. Floral art exhibit featuring the Louisiana iris 'Mrs Ira Nelson' (pp.38 & 77)

178. A champion collection of three spikes of the tall bearded iris 'Veneration' (pp.28 & 77)

179. Helen Grosvenor's champion entry in the floral art class 'By the Lake' featuring the Louisianà iris 'Margaret Hunter' (pp.36 & 77)

180. Tall bearded iris 'Lilac Lustre' bred in Australia by Les Donnell (p.79)

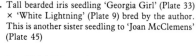

181. Tall bearded iris seedling 'Georgia Girl' (Plate 33) × 'White Lightning' (Plate 9) bred by the author. This is a sister seedling to 'Joan McClemens', seen in Plate 45.

182. Tall bearded iris seedling 'Georgia Girl' (Plate 33) × 'White Lightning' (Plate 9) bred by the author. This is another sister seedling to 'Joan McClemens' (Plate 45)

183. *(Right)* Tall bearded iris seedling 'Highland Chief' × 'Blue Petticoats' bred by the author (p.79)

184. Tall bearded iris 'Cabaret Royale' bred by Barry Blyth (p.79)

185. Tall bearded iris 'Magic Man' bred by Barry Blyth (p.79)

186. Tall bearded iris 'Bluebird Wine' bred by Barry Blyth (p.80)

187. Louisiana iris seedling 'Ann Chowning' (Plate 95) × 'Clara Goula' (Plate 92) bred in Australia by John Taylor (p.80) and now named 'Patient Reward'.

188. Louisiana iris seedling 'Ila Nunn' × 'Mrs Ira Nelson' (Plate 176) bred by Myrtle Murray (p.80)

189. Louisiana iris seedling 'Ila Nunn' × 'Mrs Ira Nelson' bred by Myrtle Murray (p.80)

190. Louisiana iris seedling 'Dural Charm' (Plate 93) × 'Clara Goula' (Plate 92) bred by John Taylor and now named 'Koorawatha'.

191. Louisiana iris seedling 'Pay Check' × 'Clara Goula' bred by John Taylor (p.80)

192. Louisiana iris seedling 'Ann Chowning' (Plate 95) × 'Charles Arny III' (Plate 114) bred by John Taylor (p.80)

9 Japanese Iris

While the tall bearded iris reign supreme in the early spring gardens, it is the magnificent *Iris kaempferi*—the beloved *Hanashobu* of the Japanese—that hold court in early summer and bring the main iris season to a spectacular conclusion. Flowers are often huge but never coarse, buds are exquisite and the partly opened flower has a beauty of its own—an equation to the 'spring' of life as we pass from the youth of the bud but have not yet reached the full 'summer' maturity of the open flower. At every stage these flowers have a beauty of their own—a beauty unequalled in the floral kingdom. While somewhat limited in colour range to white, pink, shades of blue, violet, purple and beet-reds, there is an unusually large range of patterns with self colours and others veined, marbled, speckled, rimmed, edged or dusted with blending or contrasting colours. New breaks in colour or pattern are not easy to achieve but each hybrid from a cross will give some distinctive characteristic to set it apart from all others within the overall framework. While yellow and the associated oranges, tangerines and pure pinks do not form part of the Japanese iris spectrum there is a move in that direction through crosses with the yellow English water iris, *I. pseudacorus*. The iris 'Kimboshi' (Ukei) is such a cross—yellow flowers with three falls, Japanese form and the signal areas of *I. pseudacorus*.

Cultivation

Japanese iris are very demanding in their cultural requirements and for this reason have not gained their deserved popularity. For those prepared to go to that extra little bit of trouble the rewards are great and there has been a steady increase in interest in recent years.

Japanese iris demand acid soil—a pH of 5.5 to 6.0 is desirable—and they will not tolerate lime in any form. Eleanor Westmeyer in *The World of Irises* relates the fascinating story of a German horticul-turist who planted out 10 000 Japanese iris seedlings in heavily limed soil and then intercrossed the ten surviving plants in the hope of developing an alkaline soil strain of Japanese iris. He died before completing his work.

Water is the other major requirement of these iris and while it must be stressed that they are not water plants and do not have to be grown in or near water they require copious supplies of water in the growing season from spring through to autumn. If the home gardener controls the soil conditions and water requirements spectacular results will be achieved as flowers of up to 30cm in diameter are not uncommon in good conditions. There are reports of Japanese iris growing very well in the colder areas of Victoria and Tasmania and in sub-tropical Queensland while they grow very well in the humid coastal areas and inland areas of New South Wales. They would seem to do well in any area where they are not exposed to extremes of temperature. As they are dormant in winter, frosts do not present any problem.

Japanese iris are best grown in a rich well prepared soil containing plenty of humus. This humus will enhance the water retention of sandy soils and help to break down heavy clay soils. They need protection from hot dry winds and a position that gives winter sun and either full or filtered sun in summer. I have grown them successfully in an open sunny position and also in filtered sunlight provided by overhanging gum trees. These iris will grow very well in ordinary garden conditions as long as they get ample water in spring and summer. They cannot be planted permanently in ponds or in permanently wet positions at the edge of ponds or streams. They must be given a rest period under normal garden conditions during the winter months. **Plates 152, 153.**

A very satisfactory way of growing these iris is in large pots containing a mixture of coarse sand, garden soil, peat moss and cow manure in roughly equal proportions. The iris are planted with the crowns at soil level and must be left out of water for about two months while root growth and establishment is completed. Immediate immersion will result in crown rot, lack of root growth and inevitable death. When the new shoots start to show in spring the pots can be placed in ponds or artificial ponds can be created by laying heavy duty plastic over railway sleepers and nailing down the edges or pinning them down with rocks. These artificial ponds should be filled to a level roughly 2cm below the pot level so that the crowns of the iris are always out of water. Small collections can be potted and the pots immersed in plastic ice-cream containers during the growing season.

Japanese iris should only be planted or divided in late autumn or winter and care should be taken when dividing to ensure that plants are of a reasonable size as the iris do not move readily. Because they are very heavy feeders they should be divided and replanted in good rich soil every two or three years. Plants in small pots should be potted on or divided every year while those in larger pots can be left two years. If the soil is not sufficiently acid it can be improved by adding agricultural sulphur.

Japanese iris can be propagated from seed and interesting seedlings usually result. Seed setting varies from season to season—some seasons even the bees have a great time while in others it is very difficult to obtain clean pollen to make a cross. Thrip and various pollen gathering insects will often strip flowers of pollen and a bud, on the point of opening, will need to be opened and stripped of fresh pollen to make crosses if there is no pollen on open flowers. Crosses are best made early in the morning or late in the afternoon; those made in the middle of the day are rarely successful. Humid weather seems to increase the chances of success but wet flowers usually do not set seed. A pair of thin pointed tweezers is very useful in stripping the pollen from tight anthers.

Once seed has set the swollen ovary should be left until late summer when it will have hardened, browned off and be ready to split. The pods can then be harvested and are best stored until April when they should be planted in pots containing seed raising mix. Seed left more than six months is likely to lose its viability. Germination is usually quick and there should be a fair percentage of seedlings by winter. These seedlings should not be planted out until the following April and many will flower in November and December, two years from when the cross was

Seed pod

made. Care must be taken not to plant out the young seedlings until they are large enough to survive. Apart from pollen thrip and the ubiquitous snails and slugs these iris are virtually pest and disease free.

The flower form of Japanese iris varies. There are single varieties with 3 large petals and 3 smaller petals, double varieties with 6 large petals giving a circular outline, and paeony form or super doubles with 9 or more petals and petaloids. Each type has its individual attractiveness and a selection of each type is recommended for a collection.

Single—3-Petal Types

'Asigiri' is a vigorous maroon and lilac marbled variety.

'Debonair Prince' is light amethyst-violet with darker veins and a deep violet halo.

'Fringed Cloud' is white with a blue-purple border.

'Geisha Dance' is a semi-double beauty. Short fat standards are violet red. The large falls are mid-blue, veined darker with a yellow signal and white halo and edge. This is one of the showiest of all iris, absolutely gorgeous.

'Glitter and Gayety' is a dark black-purple with a white border.

(a) Rowed-out iris planting in October; (b) the same seedlings in December

'Great White Heron' is a very large (over 25cm in diameter) pure white flower which is really semi-double with three small upright petals and three large drooping petals.

'Mystic Buddha' is an eyecatcher. The white petals are heavily edged in a dark wine-red on a flower of perfect form.

'Peacock Dance' is a great iris. Small standards are deep red-purple. Huge falls are pure white pencilled and veined red-violet. **Plate 154.**

'Shinkai-no-iro' is really a semi-double. Flowers are blue-lavender with a white centre.

'Stranger in Paradise' is a rose-fuchsia with white standards, white veins and white styles.

'Tamatsushima' is basically white with blue shading in the centre and small white standards edged in violet.

'The Great Mogul' is very dark. It is a black-purple with the most beautiful sheen when it first opens.

'Time and Tide' is semi-double and a blue-violet colour with white centre. **Plate 155.**

'Token of Friendship' is a rich red-purple with a fine white edge.

Double—6-Petal Types

'Akebono' is light rose-pink and white. It is vigorous and early flowering. **Plate 156.**

'Banners on Parade' is a rich fuchsia-red with distinctive white veins over the whole flower.

'Blue Lagoon' is a clear, plain-petalled medium sky-blue that flowers early.

'Chigogesho' is an outstanding iris. Large heavily substanced flowers are white brushed with orchid. **Plate 157.**

'Dancing Waves' is a slow growing and difficult iris but too good not to be mentioned. Perfectly formed, ruffled and rounded petals are of the heaviest substance and in a dark violet blending to mulberry colour with a white edge. If only it would grow! **Plate 158.**

'Enchanting Melody' is another in the too hard to grow but too good to leave out class. It is a wide, ruffled and perfectly rounded frilly mallow-pink with lilac styles. Beautiful but slow and difficult. **Plate 159.**

'Flying Tiger' is a late flowering pale violet with darker veins and fringed petals.

'Frilled Enchantment' is a beautiful clear white ruffled flower with a narrow rose-red border. It is a very good iris.

'Gay Gallant' is basically white with clear blue pencilling all over and dark blue-black styles giving a sharp contrast. Vigorous.

'Galatea' is a clear mid flax-blue with sharp white pencilling radiating from the yellow signals. White styles.

'Geisha Gown' is an early flowering white with rose-purple veins. **Plate 160.**

'Glitter and Glamour' has a light violet ground sanded darker with white veins. It flowers early, grows well and is spectacular.

'Hall of Marble' is an early flowering off-white marbled in royal purple over the centre of the flower and shading to violet markings on the outer edge. White styles are stippled violet.

'Hekito' is a rich cobalt-blue with white styles tipped blue.

'High Cascades' is a most unusual shade of light orchid with darker styles. Very vigorous.

'Hisikata' is a glorious iris, late flowering in deep moorish blue with prominent yellow spears.

'Hozan' is a dazzling colour and a beautifully formed iris with fluted pink-orchid petals, a white centre and white styles.

'Hue and Cry' is a plum-red colour with a white halo and veining.

'Island Paradise' has flaring white flowers edged in dark red-violet.

'Ivory Glow' is a smooth ivory-white self.

'Knight in Armour' has a light blue ground veined heavily in deep royal purple. Purple styles and petaloids. The late blooming flowers are well formed, rounded and ruffled.

'Leave Me Sighing' is a lovely early flowering bright lilac pink with yellow signals and a lilac halo.

'Mammoth Marvel' is a very large, lightly ruffled

flower in white with uniform mid-blue veining. Styles are blue edged in white.

'Mauve Opera' is a pale orchid with deep purple veins.

'Memorial Tribute' is an early flowering white with a faint tint of violet and yellow signals.

'Midnight Whisper' is a large blue-violet blend which gradually darkens from a light centre around gold signals to near violet at the edges. Delicate white veins radiate from the signals and break through the petal colour to merge with a pale rim.

'My Heavenly Dream' is a fuchsia-rose around the central gold spears blending to pink at the edge with deep red veining.

'Ocean Mist' is an early flowering sky-blue with darker blue-violet edges and prominent white centres and spreading white styles tipped blue. **Plate 161.**

'Oriental Fantasy' is a frilly ruffled white lightly sanded mauve with cream styles.

'Pastel Princess' is the most delicate shade of soft orchid-pink, almost lavender white. The well formed flowers appear fragile but have good substance.

'Pink Triumph' is a light orchid-pink with styles a blend of pink shades.

'Pin Stripe' has a pure white ground pencilled bright blue. It has tufted centres of white, and both the styles and petaloids brushed blue-violet.

'Princess Aurora' is a light mauve with a lilac-blue area around yellow signals.

'Red Titan' opens a dark red-purple and fades to aster-purple.

'Reign of Glory' is a beautiful iris. It has an intricate network of fine, delicate stippling and reticulations of sky-blue over a white ground. The colour scheme darkens towards the solid blue edges, giving an overall silvery-blue self effect. Form and growth are excellent. **Plate 162.**

'Rose Prelude' is a uniform deep rose-pink with a white area surrounding yellow signals. It is vigorous and beautiful. **Plate 163.**

'Rose Tower' is another great iris. It is a dark rosy-pink, nearly rose-red, and somewhat darker than 'Rose Prelude'. The large ruffled blooms have a white area around orange signals and are of excellent substance and texture.

'Royal Crown' is another heavily substanced iris. The flower is basically white with a large, wide beet-red-purple border. The crested white centres are enhanced with petaloids and both form and growth are excellent.

'Royal Pageant' is one of the most floriferous of Japanese iris, flowering from early in the season till quite late on well branched spikes carrying up to 6 flowers. The ground colour is pale mauve sharply veined deep red-purple. Dark purple styles and yellow signals add contrast.

'Sakurijishi' is beautiful in a clump as it gives the impression of a medley of pink shades. The clear medium pink buds open a light pink and gradually fade to near white while maintaining form and substance.

'Sea Titan' is a large lightly ruffled mid-blue of good form and substance.

'Setsu-no-homa' is a doge purple with white veins and yellow spears.

'Shinonome' is a cobalt-violet shading to almost white.

'Silken Parasol' is a clear medium blue with delicate violet shadings fading to almost white on the edge.

'Snowy Hills' is the best white Japanese iris available. The large, ruffled, snow-white flowers have golden-yellow rays emanating from the centre of the bloom. Form and growth are excellent.

'Stippled Ripples' is a dainty, frilly, ruffled flower of charm. The basic colour is white with a narrow rose-red border. Growth is excellent.

'Summer Snowflake' is a clear, gleaming white of good form and substance.

'Swirling Waves' is a violet bitone which grows and flowers well.

'Thunder and Lightning' is a dark violet-red with a blue area around orange spear signals.

'Umi-Botaru' is beautiful but slow growing. Ground colour is white, heavily stippled and marbled with bright red-orchid. **Plate 164.**

'Valiant Prince' is a lovely flower. It is a lightly ruffled rich rose-red with a small white central portion finely netted red and with styles similarly marked.

'**Woodland Brook**' is a beautiful light violet-blue with wide, gently waved petals of good form and growth.

'**World's Delight**' is a uniform, clear light pink with small yellow spear signals and pink styles giving a very pink effect.

'**Worley Pink**' is an early flowering, full, ruffled deep rosy orchid of good form and growth.

'**Wounded Dragon**' has a light base, dappled and splashed pansy-violet. Unusual.

'**Yamato Hima**' is another lovely iris. It is a pure crystal white with the palest frosty-pink at the edges.

'**Yusho**' is a wide mulberry-wine flower with white veins radiating from the centre well out into the flower.

'**Taga Sode**' is a bright fuchsia boldly veined white. It is a very beautiful, well formed iris. **Plate 165.**

'**Syucho**' is a large mauve-violet heavily veined white. Form is very good. **Plate 166.**

Extra Double or Paeony Form

There are only two of these magnificent iris readily available but each is worthy of a place in any garden. Together they present a picture of breathtaking beauty as they are as sharply contrasted in colour as possible.

'**Hagoromo**' has to be the Japanese iris to set all the standards. I cannot praise this iris enough. It has everything—glorious colour, excellent growth, outstanding form, great flower production and that one all-important property, *personality*. The flower has nine petals waved, ruffled and tufted in the most perfect rounded form. Colour is variable. Some flowers are pure white while others have variable brushings of lavender from barely discernible to heavily marked. It is large flowered and always beautiful. **Plates 167, 168.**

'**Summer Storm**' is a dark black-purple of six large petals with a big black tufted centre giving the paeony form effect. Texture is velvety, colour is vibrant and there is a dramatic air about this classic iris.

10 Other Beardless Iris

When discussing the *other* beardless iris the problem is where to begin and where to end. With over 200 known species of iris this could be a very large project, but I have restricted myself to those iris which are useful garden or water plants and which are at least available even if not readily so.

Iris pseudacorus

Iris pseudacorus, the English water iris, is a spectacular plant in every way. In suitable conditions it will grow over 2 metres high and its broad rich green sword-like foliage is a beautiful accent in the water garden. But beware! It can be invasive. The huge rhizomes multiply quickly and will spread over a considerable distance in a short period of time. I can remember planting two rhizomes, one at each end of a large natural pond over 20m long by 3m wide a few years ago. The iris flourished and each rhizome had multiplied to occupy an area covering some 20 square metres within four years. Apart from the normal intermittent sales we had to fill a large commercial order of over 1000 plants—this was done without difficulty and the offcuts and spent rhizomes were left in the pond area and surrounding path as we did not get around to cleaning them up. Within six weeks the whole area including the paths was a mass of *Iris Pseudacorus*—the plants were replenished and a small loader was needed to clear the path! If you wish to grow this iris in a pond make sure that it is contained in a pot and that the pot is strong—these plants have been known to break right through flimsy pots.

Cultivation

Iris pseudacorus is adaptable and hardy. It will grow in shallow water, at the water's edge in bog conditions or in the normal garden where its growth is not so spectacular. In early to mid-spring it produces tall, multibranched spikes of golden-yellow flowers small by comparison with the plant and fleeting. Bloom is continuous for several weeks as the multibranched spikes have double and triple flowers in each socket. I can well remember providing foliage and flowers for one of our better known floral artists to use at the Royal Horticultural Society Spring Fair some years ago—the class required height and *I. pseudacorus* certainly gave it just that. Not only did this arrangement win its class but it was the champion exhibit at the show and deservedly so.

Water is the main cultural requirement of this iris. It performs better in slightly acid soil although it is really undemanding. I have found that it can be lifted any time in our mild climate. The plant sets seed readily and the seed pods are an attractive decoration once the flowers have finished. Care should be taken to harvest the seeds even if they are not wanted as they spread and germinate easily.

As well as the normal golden-yellow flowered type there are several other forms:

'Dwarf' with narrower flexible leaves and chrome yellow flowers on a much smaller plant.

'Floraplena' has golden-yellow double flowers.

'Ivory' has pale, almost white, flowers with silver-grey veins.

'Bastardi' has sulphur-yellow flowers.

'Variegata' has variegated cream and green leaves in spring which turn green in summer.

'Holden Clough' is a hybrid of *I. pseudacorus* and possibly *I. chrysographes*. The broad flexible leaves are similar to *I. pseudacorus*, as are the flowers, which are narrower and golden-yellow heavily marked in brown-purple.

'Roy Davidson' has long-lasting, large yellow flowers for months. Spectacular new water or bog plant.

Iris laevigata

Iris laevigata is a true water iris with wide smooth foliage. It will grow in sun or part shade and demands acid soil conditions. Its behaviour and cultural requirements are similar to *I. pseudacorus* but it is not an aggressive or invasive species. There are several beautiful forms available.

Alba white with lilac tracings on the styles and falls.

'Regal' rosy-magenta with small upright standards and flaring falls.

Semperforens deep blue-violet with small upright standards and pendant falls.

Albopurpurea colchesterensis double flat flower with all petals similar in a rich deep blue with a narrow white edge on all petals. **Plate 169.**

Albopurpurea monstrosa similar to *colchesterensis* except that it is taller and a lighter blue with a less regular area and a broader white edge on all petals. **Plate 170.**

'Royal Cartwheel' similar in form to *colchesterensis* in a navy-blue-purple colour with a deep white slash down the centre of each petal.

Iris versicolor

Iris versicolor is another true water iris, native to the north-east and mid-west of the United States. This hardy iris requires the same culture as *I. pseudacorus* but it is not as vigorous. Although requiring a lot of water and quite capable of being grown in ponds or bog conditions *I. versicolor* grows well in ordinary garden conditions. The well branched spikes carry numerous buds, and seedlings are available in a wide range of colours—white, light, mid and dark-blue, maroon, light and dark purple, light, mid and dark pink, violet. There are three named varieties sometimes offered for sale.

'Claret Cup' a medium dark red-violet self with a white and yellow signal.

Kermisiana a deep purple with a white signal.

Rosea a soft pale rose-pink with a white signal.

Iris virginica

Iris virginica, very similar to *I. versicolor*, is also a United States native coming from central and south-east USA, and the two are often confused. *I. virginica* is a more slender plant with larger standards as long as the falls and is more hardy but less vigorous than *I. versicolor*. Both these members of the Laevigata family can be grown easily from seed and, as there is much variation in the seedlings, they are always of interest. I do not know of any named varieties but seedlings are available in white, grey, shades of blue, shades of pink, orchid, maroon, lilac, violet and purple. Hybrids of *I. virginica* × *I. versicolor* are available and there are reports of crosses between these iris and *I. laevigata*, *I. pseudacorus* and the Louisiana species *I. fulva*, *I. brevicaulis* and crossing of the species could be a fascinating venture for an enthusiastic hybridiser. **Plate 171.**

Iris foetidissima

Iris foetidissima is an easily grown iris for the shaded garden. This hardy iris is a native of England, Europe and North Africa and grows best in full shade where its glossy foliage is always attractive and complemented in November by insignificant flowers in shades of yellow. *I. foetidissima* can be grown in semi-shade or full sun but is a less attractive plant with increasing sunlight. The name foetidissima refers to the strong odour given off by the crushed leaves but this is not always found offensive; indeed some find the odour quite pleasant. Most gardeners, of course, do not go around crushing the leaves of their precious plants to produce unusual or unpleasant odours. **Plate 172.**

Iris foetidissima is grown mainly for its brilliant red seeds, revealed when the pods split open in autumn and which remain bright and showy throughout the winter. These seed capsules can be cut and used for spectacular flower arrangements and, if sown, germinate readily.

B.L. Davidson in *The World of Irises* reports a variegated foliage variety and another with yellow seeds but I have not seen either of these.

I. foetidissima is an easily grown plant, being easily pleased by soil conditions and not requiring large amounts of food or water. The rhizomes should be planted below the surface of the soil and can be left undisturbed for several years, during which time they will form large attractive clumps. They are best divided or planted in autumn but really can be moved at any time in a mild climate.

Iris unguicularis

Iris unguicularis is an undemanding, easily grown iris native to Algeria, Crete, Greece, Syria and Asia Minor. It is hardy and adaptable and is the only true winter flowering iris, blooms being produced intermittently in May, June and through July and August. The plants are frost resistant but are best grown in a semi-protected position, in well drained soil and are not particular about soil conditions. They require water throughout the year except in summer when they like to dry out.

The flowers come in a range of colours—white, shades of blue and violet—and as they are on very short stalks they often bloom among the foliage. For this reason the plants are best given a haircut in autumn so that the blooms can be fully appreciated. This is a fault that I find hard to forgive as I believe the foliage should complement the flower, not hide it, and a flower with foliage cut back around it really looks out of place. However the iris is easy to grow, produces winter flowers and has a most pleasant perfume particularly when cut for indoor decoration. **Plate 173.**

This iris is best planted or divided after it has finished blooming in early spring. Care should be taken to use large divisions when replanting as small pieces often do not survive. They should be planted about 1.5cm below the surface and kept moist until re-established. Protection is always needed against snails and slugs which find these flowers a real delicacy. *I. unguicularis* can be grown from seed which should be sown immediately it is harvested, whereupon good germination is obtained, but seedlings develop slowly and may not flower for three or four years.

Iris tridentata

Iris tridentata is a water loving iris native to the south-east United States. The hardy little iris requires acid soil rich in humus, can be grown in sun or semi-shade and can be grown in or out of water. If grown in the garden it requires a lot of water in spring. The small well substanced violet-purple flowers are produced late in the season, varying from late November through into December and January.

The small plants can be moved at any time but they are best divided in autumn. This iris sets seed readily and germination is easy.

Iris setosa

Iris setosa, requires similar conditions to *I. tridentata* except that it is essentially a cold climate plant, being native to Alaska and Canada. Flowers come in blues, violets and purples and are somewhat larger and earlier to bloom than *I. tridentata*.

11 Purchasing Plants

Before purchasing plants gardeners should make themselves aware of the types of iris that will grow well in their climate. In this book I have set out those species iris that are either cold or temperate climate plants, but with the hybrids, particularly of the tall bearded, Louisiana and Japanese iris, one needs to be careful in making a choice. In general most tall bearded iris will do well in cold climates and many will grow very well in temperate climates, but some will fail. Likewise, but in reverse, most Louisiana iris will grow well in temperate and semi-tropical regions but some will fail in colder climates. The Japanese iris seem to grow well over the full range of climates, but some of them are notoriously slow growers in particular areas. The best advice I can give is to discuss your selection with a specialist nursery proprietor, preferably from your own area or at least with a knowledge of your area. We have at times found great difficulty in acclimatising iris between New South Wales and Victoria, but many of the most vigorous do well everywhere.

If you wish to play safe, purchase only well established, known good doers. Of course, there is a little adventure in all of us and often the expensive new releases are a temptation too strong to resist. Purchase only from a reputable nursery, preferably a specialist or an agent acting for a specialist, and always remember that a cheap, poor quality plant takes up as much room and requires as much care as a top quality iris.

Price should always be a guide to quality and with iris this is usually no exception. New release iris in the United States usually start at US$25 (about A$28; NZ$38) and can be as high as US$50 (about A$56; NZ$76) and there is an upward trend in prices there. The nursery which imports these iris must pay for health certificates, packing, air freight, quarantine inspection and growing-on fees and there are always losses. After that the survivors are grown on for one to two years at least before being released.

New releases in Australia and New Zealand are often priced in the A$15–$25 bracket. It can be argued that they are reasonably priced when the costs

are considered. Price then is determined by supply and demand and should, in normal circumstances, decrease over the few years following introduction. Only excessive demand for high quality introductions or slow growth keep prices high. Many top quality iris can be purchased in the $4 to $6 range and specialist nurseries often put in gift iris as extras.

The best Louisiana iris have been relatively more expensive than tall bearded iris but usually multiply quickly so are initially more expensive but fall more rapidly in price. Top quality Japanese iris are not easy to obtain and multiply more slowly than either Louisiana or tall bearded iris and so retain a relatively high price.

The price of all the smaller bearded iris and other beardless iris and species is relatively lower.

Iris should be ordered early in the season as early delivery ensures satisfaction in every way. Your selections are not sold out, they are planted early and so get a good start for the next season and nurseries send out their best plants in rotation of orders.

Plants should be large, firm and disease free. Large rhizomes are well matured and in good conditions will increase quickly, while undersized plants will often need several months or even a full season to develop to flowering size. Ask the nursery proprietors if they give any guarantee. Many nurseries will offer to replace, free of charge, rhizomes of tall bearded or Louisiana iris if they are lost in the first season. This guarantee usually doesn't carry over into species iris, Japanese, Sibirica, Spurias and particularly Californians which are difficult to transplant.

A last and most important suggestion is to try to get to see the flowers in bloom during the flowering season, make your selection and place your order. If there is no specialist nursery in your area look around the gardens of friends and neighbours and get their help in making selections. Remember everyone likes to share their gardening experiences with those of similar interests and remember that if any iris does well in your district, chances are that it will do well in your garden. When you find the irises you like purchase and grow them—even wait a year for a more expensive variety rather than put in something that is inferior and will give less satisfaction. In presenting an extensive list of the best iris available I have endeavoured to make your choice a little easier. I hope that in making it so extensive, I haven't made it more difficult!

A list of registered nurseries specialising in iris appears on pages 83–4.

12 Photographing Iris

Once you have started your collection of iris the two great temptations are to hybridise them and to photograph them. As with any nature photography best results are going to be obtained by using good equipment and iris photography is best accomplished by using a single lens reflex camera, preferably with a macro lens to facilitate close-up work.

Iris photographs can be taken as portraits of single flowers, spikes, clumps or general garden display shots. A suitable collection would comprise a selection of each to give variety. The best photographs will be taken on bright but cloudy days where there is an even light overall and between the hours of 10 a.m. and 2 p.m. Suitably dramatic photos can be taken early in the morning or late in the afternoon but the colour reproduction will not always be true.

Most difficulty in obtaining true colour reproduction is experienced with the blue iris. Use of a variety of different colour films and filters did not help me but success came eventually by taking the photographs early in the morning with the use of electronic flash. Even the rich cornflower-blue of the Louisiana iris 'Clyde Redmond' was faithfully reproduced this way.

To obtain good iris photographs care is required in selection and preparation of the subject. For single blooms the flower should be at the top of the spike—with those lower down the spike part of the stem will always intrude into the photo; it should be clean, well formed, in good proportion and devoid of insect marks or holes. The subject should be square on to the frame or slightly tilted and the photographer is best positioned slightly below the plane of the flower with the sun (if it is out) behind or slightly to one side of the camera. Optimum even lighting can be obtained by the use of a reflector to fill the dark spots created by shadow. Any frame covered with aluminium foil can be used to collect and reflect light from the sun into shaded spots. The aperture selected should be such as to obtain clarity over the depth of field of the iris yet give a blurred effect to the background. This usually means shooting at f.8, f.11 or f.16 if possible. If this is difficult, use a slower speed than the normal 1/60 or 1/125 second, and use a tripod to hold the camera steady.

Spikes can be a little more difficult as you are widening the field and hence giving the opportunity for unwanted material to intrude. Watch out for that dirty piece of foliage, garden tag, length of hose or other unwanted object. Look out also for spent flowers on or about the spike to be photographed. These should be removed carefully right down to the join with the stem and any spathes moved in the process should be carefully put back into place before clicking the shutter. Position yourself in the plane of the centre or lower part of the spike. For best results never look down at a tall bearded iris; look into it or up at it. With the flat blooms of Japanese and Louisiana iris and clumps of dwarfs or Californians the best photograph is often obtained looking down or partly down into the flowers.

Clumps of iris require the same grooming techniques to ensure no spent blooms or untidy spots invade the photograph; a difficulty often experienced here is positioning the spikes to fill the frame. This can be overcome by cutting spikes in unwanted positions and repositioning them by boring a hole in the ground with a stake and placing the iris in the position required to fill the frame nicely.

With massed garden photographs precise individual care in grooming is less necessary but care should be taken to frame the photograph to give an interesting foreground and background. All of this is very idealistic and time consuming but necessary if one is to be pleased with the results. Remember the basic rule for good photography is the one word FAST:

F for FOCUS—a clear, sharp subject with an unobtrusive background.

A for APERTURE—try to work at f.8, f.11, f.16 for best results. Use a reflector to obtain even lighting.

S for SPEED—try to work at 1/60 sec. or faster, otherwise use a tripod. Photos taken at 1/125 or 1/250 sec. are rarely blurred by camera movement.

T for THINK—think about the framing of the subject, the foreground if any, the background, the grooming of the iris or irises and the positioning of the camera.

Louisiana 'Milk Maid'

'Kerries Kirtle' (Les Donnell)
Merton Calvert Award 1982; A.M. 1983. *Photo:* Les Donnell

'Wild Rice' (Harry Thomas)
Merton Calvert Award 1979; A.M. 1980. *Photo:* Henry Thomas

13 Exhibiting and Arranging Iris

This is the chapter that I hesitated about writing but exhibiting at iris shows is a natural follow-up to growing them and growing them well. Although many growers are not interested in displaying their iris at flower shows there will be many who would enjoy cutting them for floral arrangement either in set show classes or just for the pleasure of having them in the house. The iris is essentially a garden plant but no one could deny the charm of a mixed vase of California iris, the beauty of a carefully arranged bud to full bloom arrangement of tall bearded iris, the sheer exhuberance of a mixed vase of Louisiana iris or the elegance of the single Japanese iris poised with bud half open. There is certainly a place for the iris as a cut flower but transportation of any kind for the fragile open tall bearded iris is a hazardous venture.

Once a spike of iris has been selected for showing (and even in the selection there is an art as the spike must be picked for what it will be at judging time on show day, not on how it appears at the time of selection), then it should be cut as near as possible to ground level. Any excess spike can be removed at the hall in the grooming process on show day. It is often better to cut potential show bench iris on the day before the show and allow them to open inside. This eliminates weather damage to the opening flowers and makes transportation easier.

Transportation to the show hall can be accomplished by packing in long cardboard boxes, by co-opting a partner to hold the precious spikes or by placing a bucket with moist sand in the vehicle and carefully placing the spike upright in the sand.

Once at the hall the stem should be shortened to give as equal a spacing between the top of the container and each individual flower as possible. Branches which hug the main spike can be extended by using paper wads (which must be removed before benching) and all spent or badly damaged blooms should be carefully removed. When placing the treasured spike on the show bench take care to ensure that it is facing the judge and displayed to present the best possible effect. Any dirty or diseased foliage should be trimmed.

Iris are ideal plants for floral art as long as they do not have to be transported. The Californian, Louisiana, Dutch and Siberian iris all look beautiful in massed effect. The water iris, pseudacorus and laevigata are particularly effective when used with pebbles or smooth rocks while the tall bearded iris are most attractive when a few flowers of the one cultivar are used. The Japanese iris are a favourite with ikebana enthusiasts who delight in using the partly opened flower. No matter what your taste there is a suitable iris for floral arrangement and the choice is as wide as your imagination. **Plates 174 to 179.**

14 Hybridising Iris

The mechanics of making a cross were discussed in Chapter 2, this chapter is devoted more to the philosophy of hybridising iris.

Tall Bearded Iris

Hybridising tall bearded iris is mechanically easy. Random crosses will not usually result in any great advancement so a serious hybridiser should start with some aim in mind. The aim can be relatively simple—to produce an early flowering blue or a pink which grows well in a particular area or improved form in a plicata. It can be far more complex—to produce new colour patterns or to modernise difficult colours are common aims.

There are some do's and don'ts of hybridising which may help enthusiastic growers but learning is best achieved by actually doing the crosses, learning from mistakes and getting to know your iris. Some rather insignificant iris are good parents while others which have admirable qualities themselves do not transmit these to their progeny.

First let us look at what we want from an iris. The desirable traits in a modern tall bearded iris were discussed in Chapter 2. In making a cross, attention should be given to these traits and no two iris should ever be crossed if they are deficient in the same area. Inevitably if two iris with poor substance are crossed the seedlings will have very poor substance. Not only will the flaw not be eliminated, it will be emphasised. Conversely, if any iris is most satisfactory in every other area than substance there is every hope of developing an iris with similar characteristics and good substance by using a well substanced partner.

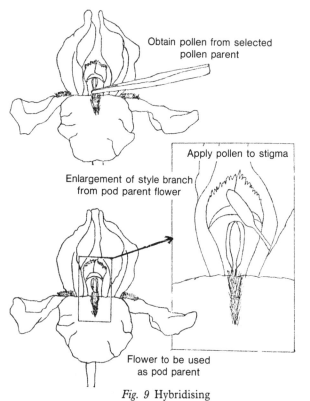

Obtain pollen from selected pollen parent

Apply pollen to stigma

Enlargement of style branch from pod parent flower

Flower to be used as pod parent

Fig. 9 Hybridising

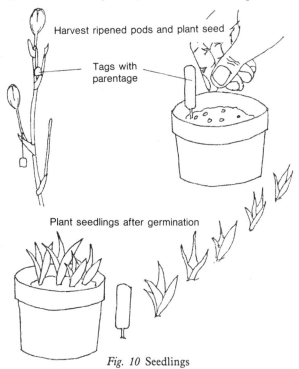

Harvest ripened pods and plant seed

Tags with parentage

Plant seedlings after germination

Fig. 10 Seedlings

Good hybridising relies on the hybridisers knowing their iris and knowing what they are looking for; even then there are many, many disappointments and, equally, many surprises.

I well remember my first really successful iris cross. For some years I had been literally fiddling around making indiscriminate crosses and getting very ordinary results. Some nice things had turned up but nothing that was better than those already around. I then decided to follow my friend and advisor Barry Blyth, the proprietor of Tempo Two Nursery and a world leader in the breeding of bicolours—differently coloured standards and falls. Barry had sent me a seedling from the cross 'Lilac Champagne' and 'Bon Vivant'. This seedling had yellow standards and blue falls. The flower form was good, the plant grew well in Sydney where many of the bicolours do not do well, the spike was strong with well placed flowers and plenty of buds. I thought the iris was worthy of a name but Barry had others more distinctive in colour pattern so it remained an unnamed seedling. Both its parents 'Lilac Champagne' and 'Bon Vivant' had standards in the yellow range and falls in the blue-violet range. Another iris of Barry's, 'Outer Limits', has beautiful colour—white standards, blue falls and red beards—nice form and good plant habits but is slow to grow. I decided to cross the seedling with 'Outer Limits' in the hope of getting some vigorous plants in the 'Outer Limits' colour range. From about 60 seedlings there was a great colour range. There were clear pinks, clear yellows, buff and gold colours, some with white standards and blue falls, some with white standards and yellow falls, some with yellow standards and blue falls, all with some good points and some bad points but none as good as the parents except one. This iris had ice-blue buds which opened to a clear pure white flower with a tangerine red beard. The branching was good, the plant robust, increase was excellent and the flower form and substance were very good. This iris was entered in the New South Wales Iris Society trial garden and has won every major award. It was registered and named 'Rellie' after my younger daughter, Narelle. 'Rellie' was the first New South Wales bred iris to win the prestigious Award of Merit. My breeding campaign had started in earnest with a red-bearded white when I was looking for bicolour patterns.

Interestingly, 'Rellie' has proven a worthwhile parent. It is a recessive white and has produced some excellent bicolours when back-crossed to amoenas and neglectas. Now, ten years after its first bloom, it is still held in high regard and is represented by an interesting breeding line. All this from chance!

It is often unwise to cross iris from the same hybridiser because the chances are that the cross has been done before, even several years previously, but I would not allow this to deter me. My very beautiful beige pink iris 'Marion Davies' is bred from two Rudolph iris ('Beige Melody' and 'Pink Angel') and yet is different from anything that Nate Rudolph has released. **Plate 40.**

Making wild crosses of vastly different colours and patterns can be unrewarding as the colours obtained from such crosses are often muddy and unattractive. There is always the chance of producing an elusive new colour but this usually comes from carefully planned breeding rather than indiscriminate pollen dabbing. If you cannot resist the temptation to try for something different, always ensure that the iris used have good substance, form, branching and plant qualities. This will cut down the number of rejects considerably. **Plates 180-3.**

There are quite a few successful hybridisers active in Australia. Iris people are friendly people, always willing to share their knowledge and experience with those of similar interests. I remember the long hours spent with Alan Johnson and Barry Blyth when I first became interested in hybridising tall bearded iris and the help they gave me. Both Alan and Barry have produced many fine iris, are excellent judges of a good iris and grow their iris particularly well. Barry has the advantage of acreage at his disposal and is professionally occupied as the owner of Tempo Two Nursery. His bicolour breeding campaign has brought him world wide acclaim and he is now actively producing fancy bicolour plicatas of excellent quality. **Plates 63-4.**

Three fascinating iris which show developments in line breeding are the Blyth neglectas 'Cabaret Royale', 'Magic Man' and 'Bluebird Wine'. In 1976 Barry released the sensational 'Cabaret Royale' with ruffled light blue standards and velvet blue-black falls accented by a bushy tangerine beard **(Plate 184)**. His 1979 release 'Magic Man', bred from 'Cabaret Royale', was taller, better formed and had a thin band of light blue around the dark purple falls. Again there was the tangerine beard **(Plate 185)**. His 1982 release 'Bluebird Wine' came as a result of the cross 'Magic Man' × 'Mystique'. Again there are the beautiful light blue standards but 'Mystique' (**Plate 66**) has given them a flush of red-violet at the midrib. The falls are dark velvety violet but the beards are white tipped mustard. By using 'Mystique' the tangerine beards have been lost in this generation but no doubt will be back in the next and subsequent generations. The form of the iris has been improved and so the line continues (**Plate 186**).

Both Barry and his wife Lesley have produced an outstanding collection of dwarf and intermediate bearded iris and their attention has now also been directed to hybridising and releasing quality Californian iris from stock produced initially by Dan Hargraves and further improved by Barry's father, Charles Blyth. This work is being continued by John Glen of Red Hill Iris Farm, who is producing Californian iris for the trade.

Top quality tall bearded iris have been produced in recent years by Rita Caldwell, Harry Thomas, Les Donnell and John Baldwin, all working in Victoria. The only serious hybridising in New South Wales in recent years has been done by the author and Myrtle Murray.

Arilbred and Spuria Iris

Sam Fankhauser in Victoria and Gordon Loveridge in New South Wales have produced some excellent arilbred iris while Gordon has also produced spuria iris of quality. Little work has been done on the spuria iris in recent times and here is an area open to an enthusiastic hybridiser. Helen Grosvenor has some lovely seedlings being evaluated prior to release.

Siberian Iris

Barry Blyth of Tempo Two Nursery has developed some beautiful Siberian iris of which 'Coolabah', 'Music Royal' and 'I'm Just Blue' are excellent examples, and the author has produced some lovely Japanese iris seedlings which will be released in the 1990s.

Louisiana Iris

John Taylor of Rainbow Ridge Nursery is a world leader in the development of Louisiana iris and his iris are acclaimed wherever they are grown. In recent years four of his iris 'Helen Naish', 'Dural Charm', 'Koorawatha' and 'Jazz Ballet' have won the prestigious Dykes Medal.

Many of Rob Raabe's iris are highly acclaimed and two that are receiving international notice are 'Sinfonietta' and 'Gerry Marstellar'. Craig Carroll and Janet Hutchinson are both producing excellent iris. Craig has the award of merit winner 'Our Parris', while Janet's winner is 'Soft Laughter'. Heather Pryor is working on Louisiana iris and producing lovely seedlings for release in the 1990s.

The future for Louisiana iris in Australia and New Zealand seems very good. These plants adapt well to climates in most areas and there is much activity in hybridising, more so than anywhere else in the world outside the United States. Already some superb creations have come from Australia and New Zealand and there is now a flow of plants back to the United States.

The actual hybridising and growing on of Louisiana iris seedlings is not easy. In colder areas they do not set seed readily but in warmer, more humid climates similar to Sydney setting seed is no problem. With the array of top quality American introductions available there is no shortage of good parent stock.

The mechanics of performing the cross are similar to those for tall bearded iris but, as there are many more bee-pods set on Louisiana iris, care should be taken to cover the crossed flower. Because of the twofold problem of contaminated pollen and insect invasion once a flower has opened, it is often best to strip a flower about to open and ensure that fresh true pollen is obtained.

Pods take longer to ripen than on tall bearded iris and here again care needs to be taken at harvest time. It seems that pods left until the skin has hardened, cracked and opened naturally produce less germination than those harvested just as the pod starts to brown off. Again the hybridiser must be careful to allow the seeds to ripen sufficiently. Some hybridisers advocate sowing the seed immediately on harvesting but I am not convinced that there is any advantage in this. Seeds planted in autumn at the same time as the tall bearded iris seeds germinate as quickly and in the same quantity as those planted immediately.

The planting medium should consist of garden soil, peat moss and vermiculite to ensure the seeds are kept moist. Seeds can be planted in pots or directly into the ground but germination is always erratic. There are several theories about seed treatment to ensure better germination but in my experience (and this is not the result of scientifically controlled tests, merely observation) no special treatment is significantly beneficial.

If seed is planted in autumn and kept moist there will be some germination within 2–3 weeks, little or no germination in winter, a further spurt of germination the following spring then little or no germination in summer. There are reports of seed germinating several years after planting but my attitude is that you want germination completed within twelve months or the hybridising becomes a burden rather than an organised pleasure. I doubt if too many serious hybridisers leave seed in pots longer than a twelve-month period.

Handling the seedlings can be very difficult because of the irregular germination as young plants are often intermixed with well established seedlings. Survival rate is low if the seedlings are planted out too early and likewise pots become overcrowded and plants rootbound if they are left too long. Time of planting is important, as again survival rate is low for summer planted seedlings. I would suggest that well established seedlings, and *only* the well established ones, should be planted out in early spring—only in September, for good bloom the following season—or in autumn, preferably during April, in the hope that plants well cared for are well established by winter and will bloom in the following October. Circumstances and the quality and development of the seedlings will always be factors but April and September are the best months for moving the young plants.

In my experience an average germination of 40% would be considered good and a growing-on rate of 80% likewise good. This means that a hybridiser can expect no more than 1 in 3 of the precious seeds to reach maturity. On the positive side, the resulting seedlings, as distinct from tall bearded iris, are

usually good and there is a very high rate of quality iris produced from crosses using good quality parents.

In evaluating new seedlings care should be taken to ensure that they are an improvement in form or colour or distinctly different before naming and introducing them. No plant should be named and introduced unless it has been well tried and has proven to be healthy. Unfortunately some rather poor Louisiana iris have been introduced, which will eventually lead to these iris falling into disrepute if they are not culled out.

The first tetraploid Louisiana iris are now available and this availability will open a new era in hybridising. Those available have stronger growth and foliage, bigger plants and larger well substanced flowers. Unfortunately the tetraploids have been reluctant to set seed and germination is even more difficult than the diploids. No doubt when more plants become available these initial problems will, at least partly, be overcome and in the future there will be an exciting range of tetraploid Louisiana iris. This is a challenging and rewarding field for any prospective hybridiser.

Introducing New Iris

Hybridisng of all types of iris is an interesting and challenging extension of growing iris. There is room for the rank amateur who merely splashes a bit of pollen around to see what will happen and also room for the enthusiast who wants to produce new and exciting iris. If you fall into the latter group, be patient; the hybridiser's skill is not learned or developed overnight but as a long range hobby it provides great rewards once you are established. New tall bearded iris hit the market by hundreds each year and many fall quickly by the wayside. There is a tendency for more and more Louisianas to be released as well. Many are not worth naming. If there is one thing I would urge to hybridisers it is to be selective in your introductions. There are too many new iris coming on the market that are not only no improvement in form, colour pattern or distinctiveness but are, in fact, inferior to others already registered. An iris should have individuality or, at least, should be an improvement on those preceding it. A good question for any hybridiser to ask before naming and releasing an iris: "If someone else offered it for sale, would I pay the introduction price of $20 or so for it?" If yes—go ahead and release it, if no—by all means keep it for your own pleasure but leave it at that.

Glossary

amoena a bearded iris with white standards and coloured falls.

anther the tip of the stamen where the pollen is found

apogon rhizomatous iris with no beard or crest—beardless iris

aril the white collar surrounding the hilum of a seed

aril-med a median iris from aril breeding

bee pod seed set naturally

bicolour an iris with standards one colour and falls a different colour

bitone an iris wth standards and falls different shades of the same colour

blend a flower showing both blue/purple and yellow/pink pigments.

chromosome the dark-staining body in the nucleus bearing genes in a linear order. The number of chromosomes is constant for a species or variety

clones a population of individual plants obtained by vegetative reproduction from a single ancestor

crest the ridge on the haft of the falls of evansia iris flowers

cross see Hybrid; Hybridisation

cultivar a variety of cultivation as distinct from a botanic variety or species

diploid a plant with two sets of chromosomes

domed standards of an iris flower when rounded and closed

dominance the quality of one of a pair or series of genes that masks or suppresses expression of others

embryo the rudimentary plant within the seed

eupogon a true bearded iris

factor hereditary unit or gene that determines the inherited characteristics of an organism

fertilisation the union of the sperm and egg to form the zygote from which the embryo develops

filament the stalk of a stamen

form the shape of a flower

gene a unit of heredity

genus the taxonomic group between family and species, including one or more species with characteristics in common

germination the beginning of growth by a seed

haft the constricted part of the standards (petals) and falls (sepals) near the centre of the iris flower

heredity the sum of the qualities and potentialities genetically derived from ancestors

hybrid the offspring of genetically unlike parents

hybridisation the formation of offspring between unlike parents

inhibitor a gene that inhibits (or stops) the action of another gene

line breeding intercrossing seedlings from the same or closely related crosses in order to improve certain qualities of a particular iris pattern

luminata a flower pattern (probably related to plicata) characterised by absence of anthocyanin (blue/purple) colouring in hafts and heart of the flower

ovary the ovule-bearing structure at the base of the iris flower which develops after fertilisation into the seedpod containing seeds derived from the ovules

ovule the egg-containing organ within the ovary of the flower that develops into a seed after fertilisation

petal one of the inner series of perianth parts (standards) of the iris flower

pH designation for acidity or alkalinity: 7 indicates a neutral condition, lower than 7 acidity, higher than 7 alkalinity

plicata a pattern of a base colour stitched, dotted and edged in a different colour

pogon bearded

recessive a trait suppressed by dominance

rhizome a horizontal underground stem

scape a leafless flowerstalk arising from basal leaves

self (colour) an iris flower with standards and falls of the same colour

self (pollination) placing pollen of a flower on its own stigma

sepals the falls of an iris flower

sheath the base of a leaf that wraps around the stem

sib (sibling) offspring from the same parents

sibcross a cross between iris from the same mating

spathe a bract or modified leaf subtending a flower or group of flowers

species generally undefinable but in practice a plant found naturally—developed without human interference.

sperm the mature male sex cell

stamen the pollen-bearing structure of the flower, consisting of a filament and an anther containing the pollen grains

standards the upper, usually broad and erect, petals that form the inner series of the perianth of which the flaring or drooping falls (sepals) form the outer series

stigma the portion of the pistil receptive to the pollen. In irises it has the form of a ridge or lip projecting from the inner surface of the style branch of the flower

stolon an elongata creeping stem on the surface of the ground

style a narrow prolongation of the ovary which bears the stigma

style crest a projection of the style branch

tetraploid having four sets of chromosomes

triploid having three sets of chromosomes

variegata the name of a diploid species with yellow standards and falls with reddish veining. Now used to describe garden varieties with yellow standards and darker (usually red-brown) falls

variety a cultivated plant (cultivar) with an identifying common name

virus submicroscopic particles that reproduce only within host cells

Sources of Iris

New Zealand

Richmond Iris Gardens
376 Hill St
Richmond
Nelson

Bay Bloom Nurseries
P.O. Box 502
Tauranga

Mossburn Iris Gardens
P.O. Box 96
Mossburn
Southland

Puketapu Iris Gardens
172 Corbett Rd
R.D. 3 New Plymouth

Ranch North
Clements Rd
R.D. 3 Whangarei

Daffodil Acre
P.O. Box 834
Tauranga

Hauauru Gardens
11 Frederick St
Carterton

Helenslee Gardens
Box 7 Private Bag
Heriot
West Otago

Waitaka Irises
Ellmers Rd
R.D. 2 Gisbourne

Australia

Tempo Two Nursery (Barry and Lesley Blyth)
57 East Rd (P.O. Box 60A)
Pearcedale
Vic 3912

Rainbow Ridge Nursery
(Graeme and Helen Grosvenor, John Taylor)
8 Taylors Rd
Dural
N.S.W. 2158

Iris Acres (Ivar and Carol Schmidt)
P.O. Box 248
Meadows
S.A. 5201

Iridescence (Kevin and Jan Nilsen)
P.O. Box 583
Cowra
N.S.W. 2794

Beryl James
Mitchell Hwy
Trangie
N.S.W. 2823

Peninsula Iris Gardens
1 Old Cape Schanck Rd
Boneo
Vic 3939

Redhill Iris Farm
34 Thomas Rd
Redhill South
Vic 3937

Iris–Daylily Display Gardens
Lot 141 Great Northern Hwy
Bullsbrook
W.A. 6084

Chaery Irises (Chris Smith)
256 Beasley St
Farrer
A.C.T. 2607

Iris Societies & Awards

Iris societies in Australia and New Zealand play an important role in fostering the growing, hybridising and eventual improvement of the iris flower. As well as the obvious social benefits, the membership of an iris society provides each member with the opportunity to learn more about iris cultivation in general and specific local problems and benefits of iris growing. Much of the information collected and stored over the years, and now written down in this book, has been as a result of the author's membership in both the local and overseas societies.

Most of the iris societies in the world have iris competitions in which hybridisers can submit their seedlings for evaluation by qualified judges. This is done in Australia by means of a trial garden system where hybridisers can submit entries for a two-year trial period. The first qualifying award is a high commendation (H.C.) certificate—if an iris does not receive this award within two years it is removed from the trial garden. Those iris gaining the H.C. remain under trial to compete for the honourable mention (H.M.) certificate during the next two years and, if successful, for the Award of Merit (A.M.) during the next two years. The Australasian Dykes Medal is awarded to the most outstanding iris bred in Australia or New Zealand after stringent testing in five test gardens located in Australia.

In addition, the Iris Society of Australia (I.S.A.) Victorian region gives the Merton Calvert Award annually to the outstanding iris in the Victorian Region Trial Garden (previous winners ineligible) and the Iris Society of Australia (I.S.A.) New South Wales region gives the Gordon Loveridge Hybridisers Medallion annually to the outstanding iris in the New South Wales Trial Garden (previous winners ineligible).

The naming (and registering) of all iris is done by the American Iris Society (A.I.S.). This society, the largest in the world, has its own system of awards starting with the H.C. certificate, then H.M. certificate, Award of Merit and finally the Dykes medal. In addition specific awards are given in each of the following categories—Louisiana Iris, Miniature Dwarf Iris, Standard Dwarf Iris, Spuria Iris, Arilbred Iris, Border Bearded Iris, Intermediate Bearded Iris, Siberian Iris, Japanese Miniature Tall Bearded Iris, Californian Iris. All iris from the United States and Canada are eligible for these awards.

The British Iris Society also has a large and complicated system of awards culminating in the Dykes Medal. These awards are given by the joint iris committee comprising members of both the Royal Horticultural Society and British Iris Society for field trials at Wesley and in London. Eligible iris are those raised in countries other than the United States of America and Canada. Thus iris raised anywhere in the world are eligible for any awards in their own country as well as the awards of either the British or American Iris Societies.

Another top international competition is the 'Premio Firenze' run by the Italian Iris Society and open to any entrant. In recent years both Barry Blyth and Les Donnell from Australia have entered and been successful in this competition.

For those interested in joining or obtaining further information about the various iris societies and the state regions of the Australian society the following list is provided.

Iris Society of Australia
and I.S.A. Victorian Region
c/o R.H.S. of Victoria
Council Secretariat
418A Station St,
Box Hill Victoria 3128
New South Wales Region
The Hon. Secretary
PO Box 11,
Gordon 2072
Western Australian Iris Society
c/- Mrs M.G. Hayes
43 Ivanhoe St.,
Morley 6062
New Zealand Iris Society
The Hon. Secretary
Mr P.E. Richardson
78 Thackeray St,
Upper Hutt
Iris Society of South Africa
The Hon Treasurer/Secretary
PO Box 82,
Bedford View
Transvaal
British Iris Society
The Secretary
Mr G.E. Cassidy
67 Bushwood Rd.,
Kew, Surrey TW9 3BG

American Iris Society
The Secretary
Mrs R.V. Ramsey,
6518 Beachy Ave.,
Wichita, Kansas 67206
Canadian Iris Society
Mrs A. Richardson,
R.R.2 Hannon, Ontario
Danish Iris Society
H. Ingemann-Petersen,
6950 Ringkobing
Japan Iris Society
17 Kitamomodani,
Miniami-Ku, Osaka City
Schweizer Iris-Und Lilienfreunde
E.R. Bronnimann,
Muhlebach Strasse,
Postfach 2618,
8023 Zurich HG
Societa Italiana Dell' Iris
The Secretary,
Palazzo Strozzi,
Florence
Société Francaise des Iris et Plantes Bulbeuses
c/- 344 Route de Grasse,
06140 Vence
The Flemish Iris Society
c/- Koen Engelen,
Herentalsebaan 126,
2228 Ranst, Belgium